AN IMMORAL PROPOSAL

Forbidden Love under Apartheid
By
Jennifer B. Graham

ISBN-10 1493613812
ISBN-13 9781493613816

For Judith and David
Cecelia, Magdalena, Phoebe, Baxter and Rory

Acknowledgements

This book has been a project two decades in the making, feeling rather like a twenty-year pregnancy. Its conception began in South Africa and since then "midwives" in different parts of the world have had a hand in its prenatal development. I owe much gratitude to Ruth Baker in New Zealand who when the "baby" lay in breech position, turned it around from novel into memoir. My thanks to Liz Hay in New Zealand for her role in its growth.

Many thanks to Sharon Stoffels, sister, friend and ally over all these years, for her support in so many ways. Much appreciation to Colleen Paulse and Marilyn Graham, in South Africa, for assisting with photo scanning and editing. A huge thank you to Una Wagner, Roger Graham and Rae Graham for their historical contributions.

To my Canadian "midwives" and cappuccino buddies Carol Drewell and Jennifer McShane, thank you for cheering me on during the final stretch. Thanks to friends around the globe for your encouragement.

And last, but by no means least, gargantuan thanks to my dearly beloved, Michael Graham whose stellar editing skills helped me birth this memoir. Moreover, without whose steadfast love there would be no An Immoral Proposal.

Contents

Prologue

I wrote this memoir for two reasons: to recount my journey in coming to terms with my family background and racial identity, and to tell my story of forbidden love.

I was born under South Africa's apartheid regime – a system where a white minority government (only white people had a vote) held absolute sway, and segregation based on the colour of one's skin was the policed order of the day. Under this political climate coupled with a fragmented childhood, my sense of belonging – where I fitted in – was a constant emotional battle.

My birth certificate classifies me as "Cape Coloured" (`Coloured` as in mixed race).

The 'Cape' part is easy to understand, that's the region where I started life, but 'Coloured'? Who are the Coloureds then?

We are a product of economic expansion. For centuries, Cape Town, at the southern tip of Africa, made trade between Europe and the Far East not just a possibility but a reality. It was the vital refuelling stop for merchant ships.

Consequently, people from many parts, both free men and slaves, came to the Cape of Africa and intermingled amongst themselves and with the indigenous San and Khoi tribes. (In those early days the tribal Africans from the north had not yet migrated that far south). Out of this miscegenation of racial groups came the Cape Coloureds.

Under apartheid there was a definite pecking order in the racial strata with Whites at the very top. Blacks, even though they constituted eighty percent of the population were at the bottom, while Coloureds were sandwiched in the middle.

Although under the Whites' yoke, we nevertheless identified with them in terms of "culture" sharing a common language, religion and even colour. For many Coloureds skin tone was all important – the lighter the better. We had no common ground with the Blacks and viewed them and their tribal customs as primitive.

While we might have seethed below the surface at the injustices of apartheid, we nevertheless accepted our lot seeing it as the more expedient choice. Collectively, we assumed the mantle Whites draped over our shoulders – happy-go-lucky, unreliable, drunken buffoons.

We are not a militant people. Besides which, trying to flex our muscle would have been sure suicide. Any ideas on our part of overturning apartheid would have necessitated our aligning with the Blacks. And then what? Whether we verbalized it or not, for us the White man's rule was the lesser of two evils.

Ironically, in the aftermath of the euphoria the end of apartheid created in the early nineteen nineties, where all people of colour rejoiced in unison, today the country has evolved into a sort of "reverse apartheid" (however much the powers that be might deny it.) Sadly, Nelson Mandela's "rainbow nation" was short lived.

As for the Coloureds, we're once again marginalised and once again "in the middle" at best, or maybe closer to the bottom rung. For all the radical political changes South Africa has undergone, the Coloureds remain in no man's land. We are a people with no real ethnic identity; no rich European history and culture the colonial White pioneers can draw upon, and no deep-rooted tribal customs and traditions the Blacks can look back to.

I grew up being told to wear my "second class citizen" badge without complaint; that I was what the apartheid government legally defined a Coloured to be: "one who *fails* to pass for White." The obvious implication being that White was superior. And being both Non-White and Non-Black connoted a double negative for us.

I was constantly reminded that we were "respectable" Coloureds - meaning we weren't *skollie* Coloureds and we weren't "primitive" like the Blacks. Respectability was defined mainly by what we had achieved materially – nice car, nice house, nice clothes.

Transgressions such as womanizing, molestation, incest, children sired in incestuous or adulterous relationships, were swept under the carpet of respectability. Conduct was about what others might think of us and how it would reflect on the family name. *"Wat sal die mense dink van ons"*

Whether we liked it or not, we had acquiesced to the White man's religious indoctrination that Non-White people were descendants of Noah's son, Ham (Gam in Afrikaans) - the cursed one. All too often, when our group behaved badly, we'd say sardonically, *"O hulle is maar net Gam"* – you can't expect any better from us.

While I don't embrace the label "Coloured" because of its negative connotation and history, throughout the book I use the term intermittently with "Mixed race" or "Brown people" for reasons of context. I've also capitalized "White," "Black" and "Coloured" to label the race groups, thereby differentiating from actual colours.

I started this book what seems a lifetime ago as a novel. It seemed safer that way because telling my story like it was, was too painful to face head on. Progress, if you can call it that, came in fits and starts. It all rang hollow and seemed so superficial. 'Why don't you write this as a memoir?' was the comment of a friend I'd asked to critique sections of my early draft. I knew then that however much I dreaded the thought, it was the only way forward, the only way to truly peel back the layers of pretence.

This memoir is not only the culmination of that long journey back but also the story of a love affair that exacerbated my struggle to come to terms with where I belong - a love affair that was not allowed to have happened.

Chapter 1

Immorality

The main road flanked by small businesses and industry teemed with dark-skinned people getting ready for their weekend activities. Convenience stores displayed attractive arrangements of tropical fruit and produce on the sidewalk. A barefooted paper boy waved copies of The Argus artfully dodging between densely moving traffic chanting, "Argie… Argie." This was the brown people's area, designated for them by the apartheid government.

Even though Voortrekker Road was bustling, Michael and I were still conspicuous in his old Chrysler Valiant on our clandestine date. I noticed he kept switching his eyes from the road ahead to the rear-view mirror.

"I think someone's tailing us," he said calmly. He was not given to panic.

I instinctively looked back and there he was, the hard-faced Gestapo-like policeman in his dark glasses and black leather jacket. We crawled along in the heavy traffic till I saw our chance to shake off our pursuer.

"Quick, turn down here to the right," I directed, pointing my finger, being more familiar with the area than Michael. My voice was steady but my heart was beating wildly. He sped up and with tires screeching swung the car abruptly. Our stalker followed suit. Michael steered the car down a side road to the right, then left. The "Gestapo" man was still there, a few cars behind us. As we approached the railway crossing, the signal began to flash red and the booms to descend.

"Keep going! You can make it!"   It was all I could do from keeping my heart jumping right out of my mouth, but externally I still remained calm. That's the way I've always dealt with crises and when over, I'd fall apart.   Michael's next manoeuvre was worthy of the best Hollywood movie stuntman as we flew across the tracks.   I turned around to see the barriers down and our pursuer blocked.

"Whew," Michael blew out the air from his cheeks. That was his way – very low key.

We made our way along the back roads to our favourite secluded beach spot. The sun was just dipping below the horizon as we pulled into the deserted beachfront parking area. Table Mountain silhouetted in the distance struck its classic postcard pose across the shimmering Atlantic.   But we were too shaken to appreciate the breath-taking vista before us.   We sat in silence. We both knew that we were playing with fire. He was my first true love, but I knew that our "love affair" was doomed right from the beginning.   I had wanted to call it off some months back, but when he begged me not to, I knew his feelings for me were genuine.

Several weeks later, we were parked again. This time under the dank, concrete underbelly of the spaghetti junction overpass.   I had resigned myself to our relationship going nowhere. I saw no way out for our predicament. It was no use prolonging the inevitable.

"We can't go on this way," I said softly, my seemingly calm disposition belying the weight of anxiety pressing down on my chest.   Michael had always treated me with utmost respect and dignity and I would handle the situation as such. After all, Mama had always taught me to conduct myself with poise, "like a lady."

"What do you mean?" he replied, gazing sideways at me from behind the steering wheel.

Concern was written all over his gentle round face just like the last time I had wanted to end our relationship.

"We have to face the inevitable, Michael. Things are just getting too dangerous. That man who followed us – I'm frightened. They're closing in on us. I can't go on like this. Let's face the facts, we have no future together."

It seemed like an eternity before he spoke.

"You're right, my darling. I know the strain you've been under and you're right, we can't continue this way. I've given the matter a lot of thought, and this is what I propose. I know I've procrastinated on a decision about our future which was remiss of me." Michael took a deep breath. "Jennifer," he began, sounding exceedingly serious. He rarely called me Jennifer, always, Jen.

"I love you and want to spend the rest my life with you. Would you come away with me to England, where we can give ourselves a chance - in freedom? I know this is asking an enormous sacrifice of you, sweetheart, to give up your country, loved ones and friends."

I couldn't believe what he had just said, and not being one to think on my feet too swiftly, I didn't know what to reply. I was dumbstruck but my expression remained deadpan. What I really wanted to proclaim to the whole world was, "Going to England? Yes! Oh yes." What I really wanted to do was to throw my arms around his neck and smother him with kisses.

But even in my euphoric state, I was conscious that embracing him in broad daylight was far too risky.

"I love you too, and I too want to be with you for the rest of my life," I said shyly.

"I can't promise you a bed of roses, my darling. You don't have to give a reply right away, but would you give what I'm putting forth some thought?"

Under normal circumstances anywhere else in the world, two people in love would pick out the best romantic settings

Cape Town's stunning scenery could afford. The man would go on bended knee, produce an engagement ring and the air would be filled with jubilation. But these weren't normal circumstances. In the eyes of the law, this was unequivocally an immoral proposal.

Chapter 2

Cape Town

"Look Mama, there's the cable car!" I exclaimed, pointing to the tiny box seemingly suspended in mid-air. "Shh, not so loud," my grandmother replied, her smiling eyes looking down at me with amusement. We were, after all, in a public bus on our way into town and one behaved in an *ordentlike* manner. And we were respectable people.

My eyes were wide with excitement as Table Mountain loomed ever closer. I was fascinated by all the details I could now see - the deep gorges and jutting cliffs of purple and blue. Trees, bushes and tracks took shape very clearly. Today was one of those crisp, cloudless days that displayed the beauty and splendour of Table Mountain, "The Old Grey Father of Cape Town," lovingly embracing the Mother City.

Juxtaposed to this beauty, the evil of apartheid was rolling in like a malevolent fog.

As a five-year-old, I was blissfully unaware of the impact this regime would have on me and my family.

Going to town resplendent in my Sunday-best dress, on a double-decker bus, no less, was a big treat. In the late fifties and early sixties, before the days of shopping malls, people dressed up to go into town – women in their coats, matching shoes and handbags, and gloved hands; men in jackets and ties, and heads topped with fedoras and trilbies

The bus groaned and hissed into its assigned bay at the Grand Parade terminal. I couldn't wait to get off and see all the goings on – today was market day. On most other days this palm-fringed rectangular block served as a public parking lot. The Grand Parade has always been at the centre of Cape Town's city life, the site of all major celebrations. From the early 1800s weekly auctions were held here on Wednesdays and Saturdays, precursors to the markets that still go on today.

The Parade bustled with vendors displaying all manner of wares - fabric, clothing, shoes, handbags, crockery, used books, vinyl records of the likes of Louis Armstrong, Ella Fitzgerald and Jim Reeves. Wafting over the throng, I can still smell the spicy aromas of curry-filled routis, samosas and other mouth-watering Cape Malay fare. But then I could think only of my favourite.

"Can I have a strawberry milkshake please, Mama?" I peeped.

"May I," Mama corrected me. "Not now girlie, when we've finished our shopping, all right?"

Hand in hand we wandered past a herbalist stall with remedies for every imaginable malady: wild dagga for 'sugar' and 'high blood,' *kwaaigoed* for asthma and heart conditions, and wild garlic for lungs. For a ten cents, the stall next door sold African wolf hairs that would bring you good luck even though it never occurred to the shoppers that Africa had no wolves. The vendor explained that if you kept a clump of hair under your armpit it would keep you safe; if you kept it in your groin area, it would bring you romance and if you kept it behind your ear it would bring you wealth.

We made our way through the jostling crowd to the fabric stall. Mama was a talented seamstress. By just looking at a piece of fabric she could see a finished garment. She fingered the navy blue linen, then began to deftly unroll the bolt extending the fabric from the tip of her nose to the end of her outstretched arm. "How much is this a yard?" she asked the honey-skinned vendor, head shrouded in a scarf.

"One rend ninety nine, merem," came the reply in a shrewish vernacular.

"I'll have two and a half yards please

"Det will be four ninety seven, tenk you merem,"

We weaved our way through the multi-coloured throng toward OK Bazaars.

Our people generally shopped at run-of-the-mill stores like OK Bazaars, Ackermans and the parade. Fancy stores like Garlicks and Stuttafords, were out of our price bracket, but it was nonetheless a treat to stroll through those sleek departmental stores with their high-end goods. Just riding the wooden escalators was thrilling enough for me.

Up ahead on Darling Street, I could hear the beat of a drum growing ever louder. We joined the crowd on the sidewalk. Mama craned her neck and smiled as I strained to look through the gaps to see what the commotion was all about. "It's the one-man band," she said glancing down toward me. We found a spot giving me a better vantage point. A dark, scrawny man in crumpled clothing and dented felt hat, his face weather-beaten, sat on a packing crate. He was clanging a pair of cymbals strapped to the insides of his knees, working a foot pedal for the drum while his toothless mouth blew back and forth on the harmonica rigged to a stand. With his hands he played the accordion. His shrivelled eyes were unseeing. I was intrigued. I had never seen such a spectacle.

"Shame," someone said, such a typical South African expression. If you dropped something someone would say shame, if the bus was full someone would say shame, if you saw a cute baby someone would say shame. Mama gave me a coin to toss in the upturned accordion case. As I did so someone said, 'Agh shame'.

We stopped in at the General Post Office – a venerable stone building taking up an entire block. The high ceilings dwarfed me, voices echoed and footsteps reverberated on the cold granite floor, unsmiling clerks used their rubber stamps like bludgeoning implements. There was something about the place that made me feel uncomfortable.

Back on Plein Street we bumped into a street photographer. With box camera at the ready he was never going to let a grandmother and her decked out grand-daughter get past him. Of the scant mementos I have of Mama, I treasure that snapshot of us standing on the granite steps of Cape Town's main post office. Me in my Sunday best dress complete with hat, bag and gloves, inquisitively taking in all that was happening around me, and Mama, a thin smile on her lips, wearing a tailored dress, peeped-toed shoes, and clutching her handbag under her bosom.

Going to town with Mama was never complete without a stop at Wellington's Fruit Growers and Confectioners. In reality it was a corridor leading from one street another but to me it was a pathway to food heaven. On either side were bins and containers chock full of all kinds of goodies - glacé cherries, plump dried fruit, burlap sacks of flour, rice and beans and delicatessen counters with varieties of baloney, salami, cheese and much more. But all I had eyes for were the candy bins – bins brimming with Liquorice All Sorts, Pic 'n Mix, chocolate covered peanuts, jelly babies, nougat, butterballs, stars, *Chappie's* bubblegum, fruit gums and my all-time favourite, melt-in-your-mouth toasted, coconut-covered marshmallow squares.

Making our way back to the milkshake stand on the Parade, we ran the gauntlet of vocal fruit and vegetable hawkers.

"Nice lychees today, merem," shouted one dark-skinned vendor missing two front teeth.

"Nice mangoes…everywhere a woman goes a man goes," he chanted in a sing-song tone. The pun, of course, went right over my head, but it made Mama smile.

With shopping bags and *Lushy* pies in hand, we headed over to the granite steps under King George V's statue, a well-known landmark on the Parade where people gathered to eat their food and soak up the sun. It was also the spot where open air evangelists set up shop. "My friend, where will you spend eternity?" the preacher's voice blared through the bullhorn. It was George MacGregor all decked out in his white-suit, Panama hat and Bible in hand. With his good looks and flamboyant style, he was always popular with the crowds. While some seem to take his words to heart, others reclined indifferently on the steps munching fish 'n chips out of newspaper wrappings; still others frowned, casting bemused glances and then wandered off.

I chomped into my steak pie with gusto. Mama glanced at me, chewing and then swallowing indicating she was ready to say something. "Tsk-tsk-tsk, mind your dress," she scolded softly without rancour tucking a paper napkin into my neckline to keep the pastry flakes off my dress.

"Now is the time to repent of your sins, come today. Georgie will sing now and while he's singing, you just come and stand right here in front of me and I will pray with you," the bullhorn blared. George Junior (Georgie) sporting side-burns and bell-bottomed pants stepped up beside his father, his guitar held in place by a shoulder strap.

Broody hazel eyes and an Elvis pout he crooned a sacred song in an Elvis voice. Young women needed no coercing for Georgie was the draw card. After George had prayed, Mama and I went forward too, but not to repent of sins.

"Hello Sister Whitman," George, whose handsome face shone with perspiration vigorously pumped Mama's gloved hand. "It's good to see you..." he exclaimed, flashing his winsome smile.

"A good turnout, hey, Brother George?" Mama's warm hazel-brown eyes crinkled at the sides as she returned his smile.

"The Spirit is moving here today, Sister. Praise the Lord!"

"Yes, praise the Lord, indeed,"

Chapter 3

Inauspicious Beginnings

We were sitting around the MacGregor's dining room table drinking tea and munching on 'Nellie's' *vetkoek*. Nellie MacGregor knew her pastries and when it came to making *vetkoek* there had been none better. She was now well into her dotage but thankfully had passed the recipe on to her children. It was on one of my trips back to South Africa that I drove Ray to see her childhood friend Lina Hoffmeister, nee MacGregor. The two hadn't seen each other since Vasco days and Lina had moved overseas several years earlier.

Before long Ray and Lina were rolling back the years reliving the moments.

Ray began to laugh as she reminded Lina of her 'big secret'.

"Yes," Lina laughed, "You were coming to see me and I was on my way to see you to tell you *my* secret!"

"What happened?" I asked, keenly interested in this conversation.

"Your mother said to me, "Lina, *ek dink ek is prregnant*! And I said to her, "Ray *ek is ook prregnant*!" In her early sixties, Lina's face was still as beautiful and her eyes as piercing and fiery as I remembered from childhood.

"Did your mothers know?" I asked.

"Ooh no!" said Lina in her slightly raspy voice. "We were so afraid of the hidings we were going to get!"

"Ooh yes!" Ray raised her voice above the cacophony of the animated conversation around the table. "I was so scared what Papa would do to me. And *joh*, Papa had a temper hey."

"And then Ray asked me," interjected Lina, "Lina *Sê vir my nou*, where does the baby actually come out? At the navel?'"

The table erupted with laughter

Embarrassed, Ray grinned, "Oh my word, I was so stupid back then!"

The news must have devastated Mama. It was common knowledge that Mama's great desire in life was to raise her children 'respectably' and see her daughters married in 'white' in the sense that wearing white signified purity. An aunt had apparently suggested "doing away" with the baby. It was a huge stigma to be pregnant out of wedlock in the 1950s. Mama firmly believed in the sanctity of life and was adamant that Ted should do the "right thing" by her daughter. The big hurdle was breaking the news to Papa. Once inflamed there was no telling how he might react. So Ray went to stay with her sister, Una, till an opportune time to approach Papa could be found.

Their courtship started on the bus. Although not complete strangers at the time, Ray knew Ted from his friendship with her brother Jonathan, it was on the bus ride they took to work each day where he began to notice her. Short of stature, he was a jovial character with soft brown eyes and wavy hair that he plastered down with globs of *Brylcreem*. Ray, a spirited nineteen-year-old, enjoyed Ted's come hither glances. The relationship blossomed and before long Ted was coming to Vasco to visit Ray rather than Jonathan. He became a regular at the Whitman's and never missed the Friday evening domino sessions where the booze flowed freely and the air hung thick with cigarette smoke. Accusations of cheating were not uncommon occasionally erupting into raucous fisticuffs.

Papa responded as expected, turning beet red in the face, eyes bulging, letting out a string of expletives and shouting, "Where is he? Where is he? *Ek gat vir hom donner.* I'll break his legs and then I'll kill him!" Ted got word that Papa was baying for his blood and wisely steered clear of the Whitman's for a while. Papa eventually calmed down and Ted plucked up the courage to ask permission to marry his daughter. Ted said he never did get an answer so they just went ahead and planned for the wedding anyway. How he got off so lightly with Papa, heaven knows.

Next-door neighbor, Tommy Burns, drove the bride and groom in his big, black Buick taxi to St. Albans church. The wedding wasn't exactly a gala occasion. There were evidently only a handful of well-wishers and Papa certainly wasn't beaming with pride as he walked Ray down the aisle. Ray's fine facial structure, thin lips, high nose and deep-set and lively brown eyes lent to her beauty. Her bump not yet visible, she cut a fine figure in her tailored beige, full-skirted taffeta dress holding a simple bouquet of mixed fresh flowers.

But prettiness was clearly not enough for Ted's side of the family. A pregnant bride was hardly cause for rejoicing. Only two from his family attended the wedding neither of whom was a parent. Social status has always been a big issue in the Coloured community. The Paulses lived in the better part of Vasco – brick homes with indoor plumbing and electricity. The Whitmans lived in Vasco's 'sticks' in a *sinkdak* home with no electricity or indoor plumbing. Papa's reputation as a drunken maniac did nothing to help. For the Paulses, Ray's pregnancy had exacerbated what was already an unwelcomed relationship. Growing up over the years I saw little of my Paulse side of the family. Get-togethers seemed to be limited to Christmas, weddings and funerals.

Five months later on 2 February 1956, Ray gave birth to me at Somerset Hospital, Cape Town. My mother doesn't remember any details of my infancy – it was all too long ago, she said dismissively. From what I'm told, the birth went smoothly - a stark contrast to what was to follow.

My parents were typical of so many Coloured people - "happy-go-lucky" lot, living only for the moment, and never planning for the future. They lived by the popular Afrikaans adage *"moenie worry nie, alles sal reg kom."* They passively resigned themselves to accept their lot of "knowing their place" in South Africa's racial landscape. They were content to put up with inferior education, menial jobs and lack of family planning. Under these inauspicious beginnings Ted and Ray's married life began with hardly two pennies to rub together.

Chapter 4

Unofficial Adoption

Only well-off Coloured people went on honeymoon then. The majority didn't because there was never any money for that sort of thing. It was out of the question for Ted and Ray. They could scarcely afford to rent a room from Ted's brother, Sidney. His home could hardly house his own family, let alone Ted and Ray. And now here was a baby adding to the congestion. Within months, no longer able to pay their way, they moved in with Mama and Papa. It was a case of out of the frying pan into the fire.

The accommodation at 107 Acre Road, Vasco, comprising a kitchen, living room and two bedrooms, wasn't exactly palatial. My Uncle Robert and Auntie Albe had to move out of the room they shared to make way for our arrival. The living room became their bedroom at night, where they literally camped out sleeping on canvas beds.

Not long after my first birthday, Ted and Ray moved across the field to Riebeek Street into one of the 'soup kitchen' terraced houses. These houses, row houses we used to call them, had started life as one big building owned by the Riebeeck Street City Mission Church and had been used as a soup kitchen. The building was later converted into three homes. Auntie Una and Uncle Koosie, and the Cupidos were Ray and Ted's neighbors.

I was left with Mama and Papa. Unofficial adoption or guardianship of children by extended family members was not uncommon among non-white people. Children were sometimes left with relatives so parents could move closer to their jobs, or simply because they couldn't afford to feed all their offspring.

As an adult, when I asked Ray why she left me for my grandparents to raise, she matter-of-factly told me that I was so cute and Mama wanted me to stay.

"But I was *your* child," I told her.

"Agh, Jennifer, things were just like that in those days," she said dismissively.

I didn't tell her then that deep inside, her decision had made me feel like a discarded rag doll. I was never unhappy living with my grandparents, but from an early age my "adoption" troubled me in the sense that I was confused as to where I really belonged.

The household now comprised the five of us. Uncle Robert and Auntie Albe reclaimed their old quarters while I slept in a single bed in Mama and Papa's room. Auntie Una had married some years before my advent and was living in one of the row houses across the field.

Chapter 5

The Kakbalie Caper

Uncle Jonathan was strong. Well, that's the way I always saw him. Not only was he strong but he was good looking. Years later, when I first saw a picture of actor Tom Selleck, I was immediately reminded of Uncle Jonathan with a similar moustache and winsome grin. He was a 'Jack-of-all-trades.' Not only could he handle a hammer and nails, he also crafted beautiful pieces of furniture. One Christmas he made beautiful miniature kitchen dressers for me and his daughter, Lorraine. Tinkering with cars was another of his passions. There was always a vehicle on blocks in front of his bungalow. Uncle Jonathan also lived at One O Seven, Acre Road. But he had his own bungalow on the property he had built for him and his family.

Uncle Jonathan, was superman. He was the hero of the hour in my toilet caper. With no indoor plumbing we had to use the outhouse. Getting there seemed to take forever. You had to take the path past the vegetable patch to the far right corner of the property by the cacti hedge. On wet days, it was a case of having to negotiate ones steps carefully hopping from one patch of grass to another to avoid the puddles. Thank goodness I didn't have to go there at night. That was what the chamber pot under the bed was for. I hated that outhouse. My mission was always to get out of there as quickly as possible. To this day I never linger in the toilet.

The lavvy was a crudely built brick edifice, slightly bigger than a phone booth, housing a wooden bench seat with a hole in the middle. Under the seat sat a large, black plastic barrel compliments of the Cape Town City Council. We called it the *kakbalie* in Afrikaans. Once a week the CCC sewage truck came by to empty the *kakbalies*. The *kakbalie* workers were the absolute ...ahem... bottom feeders of society. Errant boys were often warned by their teachers and parents that if they did not pay attention to their school lessons, this would surely be their fate.

Encountering the *kakbalie* truck, let alone working on the thing, was a nasty, nauseating business. Hapless pedestrians caught in its wake immediately grabbed for something to cover their mouths and noses, while beating a hasty retreat. On a hot day the acrid smell from the spilt raw sewage lingered for hours. Those were the days we prayed hard for rain. The chore of disinfecting the *kakbalie* with Jeyes Fluid fell on an able bodied male child. Someone had to do it – I was just thankful to be a girl.

On this particular day, as I gingerly pushed the lavatory door open. There, coiled up in the corner on the wooden seat rested a dark, brownish snake. I bounced back like a spring instinctively letting out an ear-piercing shriek. I high-tailed it down the garden path, my shrieks giving way to sobs, to my uncle who was bent under the hood of his old Jeep.

"Uncle, there's a snake in the lavatory!" I wailed.

Mama came rushing out the kitchen door, my bare-footed cousins, playing in the yard dropped everything and came running toward me.

Uncle Jonathan grabbed a nearby spade and marched to the loo like a military commando, the rest of us following him like an infantry unit. He cautiously pushed the door open with the blade end of the spade, took a step forward and began flailing away furiously. Suddenly all was quiet. Uncle Jonathan backed out of the loo. His face cracked into a triumphant smile as he showed off the decapitated snake draped limply over the spade. Its severed head besides its slithery body no longer posed any threat to neither life nor limb. The cousins gawked at the reptile, pointing in fascination.

"It's okay, you can go in now," announced Uncle Jonathan with all the confidence of a war general who had just rescued the village from its deadly foe.

"No," I cried, still wracked with fear clinging onto Mama.

"Look, the snake's dead," my uncle reassured me as I eyed the two pieces suspiciously. With the cousins in tow, he carried its remains to the backyard hedge. It took some coaxing to get me back into the loo. No sooner was I perched on my haunches on the wooden seat, than a lizard darted along the wall, scaring the stuffing out of me. This was no time to linger and pull off a square of "toilet paper" – sheets of newspaper impaled on a six-inch nail. I leapt off the seat in terror and ran crying to Mama. She eventually got me to do what we usually did with the paper – rub it between our hands to soften it and then perform the necessary.

Chapter 6

Domesticity At One O Seven

"Bless this house, O Lord, we pray, make it safe by night and day…" Mama's soprano voice rang over the rhythmic clatter-clatter-clatter of her old rickety hand-crank Singer sewing machine. "Old Faithful," she called it. I sat on the oilcloth floor gathering up scraps of fabric off-cuts Mama dropped, draping them over my doll.

One O seven, Acre road, Vasco was a humble dwelling but Mama kept it immaculate. Like any respectable 1950s housewife, she prided herself on running a clean and scheduled household. She was not one to be idle. When she was not cooking and cleaning, she beavered away on sewing assignments. She designed and sewed tailored suits, dresses and bridal wear for wealthy people in the white suburbs. Good Coloured seamstresses were their weight in gold among white ladies of means.

Mondays were *bobotie* days. Out would come the cast iron meat grinder which Mama would screw to the edge of the old kitchen table. Then came Sunday's left-over roast from out of the safe. I have no idea why it was called the 'safe.' It was a kitchen pantry cupboard with a wire mesh front where the butter, leftover meat and other fresh food were stored. We had no fridge, we had no electricity. On the wooden chopping board, she methodically cut the cooked meat into cubes. I stood by grinder waiting for Mama's signal.

"All right girlie."

I eagerly grabbed the grinder handle with both hands and cranked away with all my might as she fed the meat into the chute. I never tired of doing it. I loved watching the meat forming curls as it squeezed through the holey plate bit. Mama would then add the ground meat to onions sautéing on the stove, seasoning it with curry powder, vinegar and sugar. To this she mixed in milk-soaked bread, transferring the mixture to a buttered oven-proof dish. She'd then pour a savory milk and egg custard over it, add a few knobs of butter, finishing it with a fine grating of nutmeg. Then it was into the oven with this traditional curried, sweet and sour dish. I don't even have to close my eyes today to see that old wood-burning range with its rectangular gauge that read 'warm, moderate, hot and makers name emblazoned on the front – Welcome Dover.

I knew her as Auntie Sophie. She was no blood relation, but as a mark of respect we always called our elders auntie or uncle. Every second Monday she came to help Mama with the washing. I swayed back and forth languidly in the tire swing under the mulberry tree watching Sophie leaning over the galvanized tub by the outside tap. Auntie Sophie was to laundry what Mary Poppins' Bert was to chimney sweeping. 'Chee-cheecheechee – cheecheechee – chee,' she rubbed the blue-soaped garments back and forth between her hands in the water producing a syncopated squeaky sound. The bangles on her arms jingled musically. She was the original "one-man band."

Bed sheets and white shirts got an added cube of *Blue* dissolved in the water for extra whiteness. Auntie Sophie ran the sheets through a mangle before spreading them over the bushes to dry. The shirts and other clothing were pegged onto the long clothesline in the yard. I used to picture my hands caught between the mangle's rubber rollers and my arms coming through the other side pressed flat in cartoon fashion.

"Coo-ee! Come have some lunch! "Mama's voice sounded down the pathway. "Holly-ha, Mrs. Whitman, is it that time already?" Sophie exclaimed, revealing two gold incisors. Just then a couple of next door's fowls sauntered into our yard their heads jerking back and forth, eyeing us askance. They nonchalantly began scratching in the dry dirt.

"Shoo! Shoo! Shoo!" Sophie shouted clamorously waving her arms. The chickens scattered, cackling frantically as they darted back through gaps in the cactus hedge separating us and the Alexanders.

"They such a nuisance, man," Sophie said addressing me. "They scratch in the dirt and will get the washing dirty." Nature had given her high cheek bones naturally rouged, lending her skin a honey glow.

"Come Jannity," she beckoned me. For some unbeknownst reason, that's what Sophie always called me.

"Come, let's go have some lunch. Your granny makes *lekker* bread, hey?"

As I caught up with her, she glanced at me through twinkling eyes, saying,

"You getting big, hey?" Pulling my shoulders into a shrug, I looked at her shyly grinning as we walked down the path to the kitchen.

As always Mama didn't disappoint - delectable roast beef and beetroot sandwiches and a pot of tea.

"Alexander's chickens came to scratch by the bushes again, Mrs. Whitman. I chased them away."

"Tsk,tsk,tsk," went Mama, crossly. "We're having such trouble with the Alexanders and chickens, man. Two of ours went missing, and Jonathan is convinced Lloyd kept them when they wandered into their yard. And you know what he did? He dyed them brown!"

"Holly-ha, Mrs.Whitman!" Sophie hands sprang up to her cheeks. "But how can he do that?"

"Oh, that Lloyd is such a *skelm*," Mama retorted.

"*Haai*, how can he be so *skelm*, man?" Sophie responded with incredulity, the humor of the situation completely lost on us.

"The washing on the line should be about ready for ironing," Mama remarked, draining her tea.

"Yah, and the sheets are nice and dry already," Sophie replied rolling her 'rs' in the typical South African manner of speaking. The old fashioned flat cast irons sat on the hot stove.

"Right y'are, Mrs. Whitman, I'll just go finish up the last of the washing then and then I'll do the ironing."

"Thank you, Sophie."

"Right! Now for the dishes," Mama declared, rising from her chair. She placed the large enamel basin on the kitchen table into which she poured water from the enamel pitcher.

"You come help me dry the dishes, girlie."

I took the tea towel from its hook by the stove and waited, pleased to be helping my Mama.

The Alexanders lived on the corner of Flinders Street and Acre Road. Then came us at One O Seven, and then the Burnses. The Alexanders were hawkers. Their yard was always a busy place - neighing horses, crowing roosters, a braying donkey and men and boys loading the horse cart with fresh produce. Lloyd would take the horse clip-clopping down the streets of Vasco selling fish, fruit and vegetables to housewives.

Tuesday was fish day. "Whoo-whoo-whooo," the ram's horn sounded. I can still see the lifeless silvery fish, eyes glazed neatly piled on the back of Lloyd's cart. The blinkered old nag stomped her hooves on the gravel kicking up small puffs of dust. I jumped when she suddenly blew loudly through her nose and lips. I looked enviously at her long swishing tail. If only my hair would grow that long and straight.

"What you got today, Lloyd?" Mama asked, as Lloyd pulled up in front of our gate.

"Maasbankers and stockfish,"

"Are they fresh, Lloyd?" asked Auntie Burns, our next door neighbor, joining us with her arms wrapped around an enamel basin.

"Got them from the market early this morning," said Lloyd, all business-like.

"I'll take a pound of stockfish, Lloyd," Auntie Burns said." While Mama bought maasbankers Lloyd thanked the women, pocketing their payment. "Tsk, tsk," he uttered, tugging on the reigns, setting the horse clip-clopping down Acre Road. "Whoo-woo-whooo," the ram's horn wailed again.

"Coming over for a cuppa tea, later Minnie?"

"Okay," Auntie Burns replied, "Just want to get the washing on the line while the sun is still high."

The Burnses were like extended family. They had three sons, and a daughter, Gracie. Gracie was my Cousin Connie's playmate and I just tagged along. We were back and forth in each other's yards playing *housie-housie*, and aunties sipping tea. Minnie Burns had watery blue eyes, straight hair and a fair complexion. She was descended from a well-to-do White family, so Gracie told me a few years ago. Her White grandfather had married a Coloured woman and was promptly disinherited. Although this was decades before apartheid became law, interracial marriage was nevertheless the exception rather than the rule and was regarded as a blot on the family history by the White relatives.

Tommy Burns had shiny, dark chocolate skin, a rough bulbous nose and an amazingly pink tongue, just like the colour our tongues turned when we kids sucked on Stars' taffy. Mr. Burns was no oil painting. Perhaps it was his neon pink tongue women found irresistible because it was no secret that he was an unabashed philanderer. He loved *jolling* with pretty women in his taxi.

Over cups of tea, Minnie Burns would have Mama's sympathetic ear as she lamented about her husband's transgressions. Gracie and I would try to eavesdrop. "Shoo! You two go play outside!" Mama would say, followed by the phrase, "*koppies het ore*" (teacups have ears.) I always wondered what that meant.

Chapter 7

Mama

It was pretty much a given in our community that almost every family had skeletons in their cupboards. But it was also true that it was very difficult to ferret them out. Respectability was a very important virtue in the fifties and this extended to family history. Never mind that one has no control over one's ancestry, somehow, the Cape Coloured people deemed it important that their lineage be nice and 'clean' – no murky past.

In truth most of us are only a few generations away from our slavery roots, but we love to imagine that the cherished 'white' in us hale from upright and, dare I wish, noble stock. And these are the very people who, until Nelson Mandela came to power, ruled the roost over us. We are indeed a strange people. I have never met a Coloured person who championed his non-white heritage.

In true fashion of the times, Mama sheltered me from the harsh realities of my family history. It has only been since I've delved into my genealogy that under the veneer of respectability some nasty blemishes have come to light. No one dared talk about taboo subjects such as divorce, children born out of wedlock, infidelity, incest and violence. Because, after all, they just wouldn't be the sorts of things that would happen in our family.

Mama was a demure, coquettish, romantic woman who would probably have been much at home in the Edwardian era. In her handbag she always carried a clean lace-trimmed handkerchief and a bottle of *Eau de Cologne* in case someone came over faint. She was a stickler for manners and etiquette. Her first husband, Daniel Hartzenberg, of whom nobody spoke, was Auntie Una's father. I was in my late teens before I came to know that Auntie Una and my mother were half-sisters. I didn't even know that Mama had been married before. It was only in later years in talking to Auntie Una, I found out about Mama's first marriage.

Auntie Una described her biological father to be a dark-skinned Indian-featured man, who converted to Islam and took on the moniker of Salie. Evidently, during courtship he was attentive and charming, but after they were married, he became extremely controlling over what Mama wore and whom she befriended. He demanded that his clothing be laundered in a specific way and that she give an account of her day while he was away at work. He was apparently a very vain man and competed with Mama in terms of appearance. After Una was born he lost interest in Mama and made no secret of his philandering behaviour. According to Una, he was very possessive of Mama and discouraged her from paying her daughter any attention. Mama divorced him when Una was four years old.

Mama's mother, Magdalene Kemp, a midwife, dark-skinned, short, fat, and evidently formidable was known to everyone because she was always remembered wearing her white starched nurse's veil. John Kemp was her stepfather, but regarding her biological father there seems to be some mystery. Speculation has it that he may well have been white based on her light skin tone, hazel eyes and thin lips.

As it was with American slave masters fathering children with their female slaves it wasn't uncommon in colonial South Africa for white men to sire children with their servants. The burden inevitably fell on the mother to bear the consequences – the white father almost always abdicating any responsibility for his actions, a practice that was perfectly acceptable with many in the White community.

Mama had a roguish, one-legged brother, John, known to all as *Boeta* Jawn. Whether the sibling connection was on the paternal or maternal side is again one of those mysteries or at least was a well-kept secret. Mama seemed not to associate with him, especially when he was inebriated. Occasionally he would shuffle through the door on his grubby crutches and plonk himself down at the kitchen table no doubt in need of food. Mama never begrudged him a cup of tea and a sandwich. I was oblivious to his being any relation to Mama. I thought she was just being kind to a vagrant. His features were rough, like he'd been in a few dogfights. His hair resembled steel wool and he had a sour smell about him. I regarded him with great suspicion and always gave him a wide berth whenever he came to the house.

Once or twice I went with Mama to deliver food parcels and Papa's cast offs to Boeta Jawn. We would walk down Acre road past Riebeeck Street, past Mrs Prodgers shop, past Janjeera's shop and there in a field was Boeta Jawn's shack. He lived in a one-roomed windowless, corrugated iron hovel furnished with a single camping cot resting on a dirt floor. A stale smell of body odour, tobacco and urine permeated the *pondokkie*. For me it was a spooky place. I'm glad I didn't go there too often.

Chapter 8

Don't Bring Out The Scots In Me

When Papa got mad, he got bloody mad. Whenever angry, his face would flush, his neck would turn red, his eyes would bulge and he would thunder in a menacing tone, "Don't bring the Scots out in me!" Papa was fiercely proud of his supposed Scottish ancestry. Although nothing tangible existed about his heritage, it took a brave man to challenge him on it. According to Papa, his father, John Whitman, was of Scottish decent. He had died of 'fever,' when Papa was about twelve years old. His sister Ruth remembered very little about their father as she and her brothers were too young but was unaware of any Scottish roots.

When he had a drink it was like a legion of demons besieged him and caused him to wreak havoc in the home. Mama and the children often fled in terror. The more I heard of Papa's outrageous behaviour, the more I wondered how she could ever have married him, especially as she was such a lady. Knowing now a little of her first husband, I can only conclude that she had some fatal attraction when it came to men.

Papa would beat the children over the least infringement - when chores weren't properly done, when one pouted about having to do them, when he didn't get a "Yes Daddy" answer to a command. For good measure, the children had to pick their own implements of punishment - switches from the quince tree.

On my visit to Cape Town in 2004, speaking to those who had known Papa in his earlier years, the one common denominator in all their accounts was his legendry temper. I found this both very disturbing and perplexing. Disturbing because of the brutality of the man, perplexing in so far as the Papa I knew growing up in Vasco was a benign gentleman. Yes, he had his idiosyncrasies and he certainly could be stubborn, but so violent?

My Uncle Jonathan, well he didn't look quite so strong any more, the Tom Selleck looks had faded, and his hands shook from Parkinsons' Disease, recalled the time it took him two hours to get Papa's newspaper. Papa had sent Jonathan to the corner. On the way there, Boeta Jawn waylaid him and sent him on an errand. He didn't have the nous to tell his uncle he was in the middle of doing something for his father. Children were trained to blindly obey their elders.

When he returned to Boeta Jawn's shack, his uncle persuaded him to sit down and taste the concoction he had brewed up on his primus stove. A couple of hours went by before Jonathan eventually got to the shop.

"Man, Jenny, when I got home I knew I was in trouble."

Papa yelled at me, 'Where the hell have you been?'

I just said, 'To the shop, Daddy,'

He shouted back, 'It takes you two hours to go to the *blerrie* shop, hey?'

You must know Jenny that his face was all red, now I was scared, man.

I told him Boeta Jawn asked me to go buy him a chicken at the butcher shop.

"Never mind Boeta Jawn! When I send you to the shop, you go to the *blerrie* shop. You don't go run around for Boeta Jawn, do you understand?'

All I could say was, 'Yes Daddy,' "Then he told me to go get the *lat.*

I knew what was coming, man so I tore just a thin *stukkie* off the tree. He grabbed that branch from me and chucked it on the ground. He *klapped* me so on the back of my head. He got himself a good size *lat* from the quince tree. I stood there waiting for him to come back inside already crying. 'In you go,' he pointed to that small bedroom; you remember that one just off the kitchen. Man, then his hand came up way high and he brought that *lat* down so hard I'm telling you. And then another one, and another one".

"But didn't you try to defend yourself or get out of the room," I asked in dismay.

"Man, I couldn't get out. The door was closed and I was trapped. I moved around the room putting my arms over my head and trying to cover my body as best I could".

"Did the *lat* cut into you?"

"Yes man. Those *latte* made, what you call it … stripes."

"Welts?"

"Ja man. Papa had that wild look in his eyes. Then he says to me, 'Yes, you dance, boy!'".

Uncle Jonathan tried to mimic the action in slow motion with his arm.

"'Yes, you dance, boy! Next (whack) time (whack) I (whack) send (whack) you (whack) to (whack) the (whack) shop (whack) you (whack) go (whack) straight (whack) to (whack) the (whack) shop (whack), do you hear me?'"

"Where was Mama all this time," I asked in bewilderment.

"Jenny, you must know that when Papa was like that, you stayed away 'cause you could be next."

But a mother can bear just so much however much she may believe in the Biblical adage 'spare the rod and spoil the child.' The howls and despairing sobs coming from the room left her no choice but to send Ray to go and get Mama Lenie Baptiste, Papa's mother.

"Mama Baptiste opened the door and uttered loudly, 'Stop! Enough', and Papa just stopped

Ray chimed in, "Yes, Mama Baptiste said 'Why did you have to beat the child half dead?'" Ray recalled that Papa was still panting and his face was all wet with sweat, and he just said, "That will teach him to do as he's told."

Mama brought Jonathan sugar water to drink as he lay in a helpless heap on the floor. His arms and legs were covered in welts, the shirt on his back stained with blood. Mama put some ointment on his back which he said, with a wry smile, hurt almost as much as the beating.

Jonathan didn't attend school for a few days because, in his physical state, he would surely have been reported to the Children's Welfare authorities. Strange as it may seem the apartheid government did extend some degree of child protection to the Coloured community. No doubt Mama was protecting Papa from the consequences because she was afraid of what he might do to her let alone the shame on the family if he went to jail.

"How old were you, Uncle?" I asked.

"Man, I suppose I was about ten".

"You must have really hated Papa"

"*Agh* no Jenny, man. That's just the way things were in those days," Jonathan replied in a matter-of-fact manner that left me speechless.

I learned later that Mama Baptiste was the only one who could calm Papa down.

Mama and Papa Baptiste lived just down the road from us in a brick house with a long cool veranda with porthole windows. Mama Baptiste was a feisty woman; in contrast Papa Baptiste's toothless, benign character. He always looked like he had something to say, but was never given the opportunity. Whenever we visited them, he always hovered in the background. I never saw him without a jacket and tie. Reminiscing about the old man, my relatives chuckled about his wearing a jacket and tie even to the beach during holidays.

Now and then Mama Baptiste, walking cane in hand, would shuffle over to our house for a cup of tea. I never really liked her. She had a face that could turn milk sour. Even as a child I could tell she didn't like children. The Baptistes had geese in their yard. I didn't like going over there because the honking geese would come chasing after me. Their behaviour always reminded me of Mama Baptiste – unfriendly and unwelcoming. Whether it was my imagination or not, it seemed to me that her very cadence was goose-like.

"Was Jonathan the only one who Papa was so terrible to?" I asked.

"He never beat me," replied Auntie Una. But the others all got a hiding, even poor Albe who never did anything wrong. But your mother got most of it," replied Aunt Una.

"Was she the naughtiest?"

"Not so much naughty, but more defiant than the rest of us.

"Ooh, there was the time I laughed so much." Auntie Una was on a roll. "Ray's job was to pack our school lunches and also Papa's sandwiches for work. He saw her cutting the bread skew and smacked her sideways on her head.

"'I can't help it, Daddy,' Ray says."

"'I'll show you how to cut the bread straight', but you know Jennifer, it was stronger than that but I'm not going to say it like Papa did. Then he started taking off his belt. But Ray was smart. She ran out of the kitchen door with the knife still in her hand. Papa goes rushing after her and Ray starts running round and round the house."

Everyone chuckled.

"Papa's pants started to fall down," Auntie Una continued.

Knowing the layout of the house, I wondered why it had never occurred to Papa that he could have taken a short cut through the house to catch her. It was obviously Ray's lucky day.

"I never knew why your mother took so many chances when she knew what a temper Papa had," Auntie Una said wistfully.

"Shame," Auntie Una continued, in her melodic voice, "One time Papa punched your mother in the mouth."

"Wow," I responded quietly, not being able to fathom such violence.

Ray was washing the dishes when Papa noticed a speck of food on one of the dinner plates draining on the metal tray.

"Papa picked up the plate and shouted, 'Look at this! When you do a job, you do it properly. Just for that, you do the whole lot over again. Your mother made it obvious she didn't like this - she pushed out her lips in a pout."

"How old was Mum then?" I interrupted.

"Let me see," Auntie Una replied, pausing briefly. "Man, she was about ten years old. Ooh, I'll never forget the way how Papa got so angry, his eyes almost popped out. He screamed at her, 'Don't you make *dikbek* at me, my girl.' Jennifer, he hit her in the mouth with his fist."

I couldn't believe what I was hearing - such wanton rage and violence?

Papa had actually knocked her cold and it took smelling salts to revive her.

"I can remember bringing the water bucket so she could wash out her mouth. She started to scream and scream when she saw all the blood".

"And Papa? What did he do?" I asked incredulously.

"He just walked away, he didn't say anything. Your mother was never quite the same after that."

Auntie Una remarked that over the days that followed, as the time approached for Papa to arrive home from work, Ray would become distraught, wail and cower in fear. Coloured people seldom went to the doctor. They would rely on old wives remedies for all kinds of maladies. Besides sugar water, there were always the trusted old *Hollandse Medisyne* of which

Versterk Druppeltjies were staple for nervous conditions or shock. Any psychological condition fell under the umbrella of "nerves."

Chapter 9

Just The Way Things Were

When Ray's state of health deteriorated, Mama wrote a letter to her aunt up country asking if Ray could stay with her for a while. The 'while' lasted five years! I visited Auntie Minnie's house once with Mama and Papa. I was about seven at the time. We went on the long road trip in Papa's pride and joy, his dark green Studebaker. Auntie Minnie lived in Buffelsjag, a remote *dorp* in the Western Cape Province. Such trips were a rarity so for me this was one big adventure. Mama packed biscuit tins of *padkos*. What few restaurants there were along the way weren't for us. They only catered to a white clientele.

It was still dark when Mama woke me. I knew it must have been very early in the morning because the roosters weren't even crowing yet. The air felt crisp against my sleepy face when I went outside. I rubbed my bleary eyes as I tumbled into the back seat while Papa arranged the last of the luggage in the boot (trunk) by flashlight. Mama looked back and smiled at me while I snuggled under the blanket, resting my head on the pillow.

The headlights cast twin beams of light against the pigeon coop next to Uncle Jonathan's bungalow. Backing the car was always quite a performance with Papa. He would slip the gear into reverse, and with one arm on the steering wheel the other resting on top of the front passenger seat, he would begin to grunt and groan as he slowly let out the clutch. And this kerfuffle would continue all the way down the driveway.

We drove through our slumbering neighbourhood to the National Road. The soothing, soporific hum of the car engine soon sent me into dreamland. When I eventually opened my eyes, the sun was high in the sky and we were driving through a patchwork quilt of undulating orchards and vineyards. I don't know how long I slept but soon after waking I was pretty hungry. It seems like forever before Papa finally spotted a picnic table where we could stop for breakfast. In those days a roadside picnic spot comprised a lone concrete table and bench. You'd be lucky if you found one under a tree. And if it was occupied, there wouldn't be another for miles and miles. At least the saving grace for us was that the government hadn't demarcated these spots as "Whites only."

Could Mama ever pack a picnic – beef and beetroot sandwiches on home-made bread, cream crackers and cheese, hard boiled eggs, meat pasties Mama had made from scratch, home-baked cookies and cakes, candies, flasks of tea and coffee and Oros orange cordial. Post-picnic ablutions had to be performed behind the bushes as toilet facilities weren't available for non-whites. On the road again, to pass the time Mama and I got into sing-songs and sometimes Papa would join in whistling.

As we past the Swellendam sign, I became acutely aware of a distinctive and refreshing aroma I later came to learn that this aroma was peculiar to that area and emanated from the bracken, heather and *fynbos*. It was such a natural, pleasing herbal scent, in such contrast to the smells of the big city.

"Not far now," Mama said, turning her head to look at me. Shortly after the Buffelsjag River sign we turned off onto the gravel road to Auntie Minnie's house. 'Not far now,' seemed like forever to me. We drove and drove along the lonely dirt road, our car kicking up a trail of dust in its wake as we passed arid scrub land dotted with whitewashed farm workers' cottages.

And there it was, a diminutive cottage flanked by an enormous rainwater tank dazzling in the hot sun. Auntie Minnie and Uncle Johnnie stepped from the dark interior using their hands as visors against the white sunlight, as Papa brought the Studebaker to a halt under a shady tree.

"We saw you way *daar doer* in that dust," remarked Uncle Johnnie, a thin, swarthy man with a ready gappy smile.

"Hello *hartjie*," Auntie Minnie smiled down at me.

With greetings and kisses done, we entered the low door into the cool, dark kitchen that reminded me of one of Beatrix Potter's anthromorphic burrows. Auntie Minnie's shelves were neatly stacked with preserved peaches, guavas and pears. They made my mouth water. What was very different to anything I'd seen before, was her kitchen floor. It was hard, shiny and looked like cork. When I learned later that it was cow dung my immediate reaction was 'eeuw!' I was surprised it didn't smell at all. In the country, cow dung had many uses besides fertilizer and was commonly used for flooring.

This is where my mother came to stay as a young girl for her convalescence.

Years later, when I asked her what it was like at Auntie Minnie's, she replied "Man, Auntie Minnie could be *kwaai*...I had lots of chores to do. If I didn't do them when she wanted them done, I would get a hiding." I detected a certain sadness in her voice.

"What kinds of chores did you have to do?"

"Oh, sweeping the floor, dusting, doing the dishes and fetching water in the bucket from the dam, you know?"

"What was the water used for?"

"For cleaning and bathing."

"And the rainwater in the tank was for drinking?"

"Yes."

On our visit I had walked that same beaten, pebbly path to the dam, but not to draw water. I had the luxury of sitting beside the dam tossing in stones, the plop breaking the conspicuous stillness. Little did I know then that my mother had trodden the same track to the red muddy water, and had most likely played under the same trees. It was under those selfsame trees that I played this bizarre "funeral"game. I had a Kewpie doll I didn't much like and decided to hold a funeral for her. I used a small box for her coffin and used other small boxes as cars for the cortege. I dug a hole in the arid ground and buried her. I felt neither sad, nor happy. In retrospect, the funeral game was very likely a part of my coming to terms with my Auntie Albe's death some months before.

During her years with Auntie Minnie, Ray said she had to walk for miles to the small school and couldn't relate to the country children. She missed her old teacher and classmates in Vasco. She was lonely and heartsick, often sitting by the dam crying for Mama to come and take her home.

"Why did Mama leave you for such a long time?"

"I don't know," she shrugged. "That's just the way things were".

My mother's reaction reminded me of the way Uncle Jonathan responded when I had asked him about Papa's abuse.

Chapter 10

Turning Point

Ted was one of eight children. Their family ethos was typical of many Coloureds – the more children you had, the more the collective income and the better the assurance of old age security for the parents. In the only correspondence I got from Ted after I had left South Africa, he wrote:

> *"Having been the son of a labourer and of colour in this country has never been a bed of roses. However my parents reared me in hard times to the best of their ability. I always as a child had ambitions and dreams for the future. In spite of our plight and situation, I wanted to be a school teacher but was robbed of the opportunity."*

He had to leave school at age fifteen to contribute to the family coffers. He had a good mind, but without the opportunity for higher education, he couldn't realize his full potential.

Apartheid ideology stifled such ambitions. Whites got preferential treatment and amenities. Being uneducated, many Non-White people bought into the church's teachings of Non-Whites' subordination to Whites – being good only for menial and domestic employment to benefit Whites. Religious-oriented Coloureds of that era were brainwashed by the church. "The Bible says we must obey our government leaders." We were told we are Ham's descendants. This is our lot. Our reward is in heaven.

From early on soccer was Ted's passion. He lived for weekends. Saturday was the day of the big games. Blackburns' home ground was the field owned by Tommy and Minnie Burns behind Mama and Papa's house. Fans turned out in droves. 'Go Blackburns, go Ted, go Blackburns, go Ted', they chanted. He was Blackburns' rising star.

Marriage and a family didn't diminished his enthusiasm for the game and the time he devoted to it. Ray was an occasional spectator, she wasn't really into soccer. And Mama didn't make it any easier. She didn't like her daughters watching the games. She said it was unladylike for women to be jumping up and down the sidelines making spectacles of themselves. And she resented the rowdy crowd virtually on her doorstep.

I too was an occasional onlooker although I never understood much about the game. I would generally hang around the fringes of the cheering throng, occasionally squeezing my way to the front. But the effort was never worth it, in fact it was upsetting. Here were bodies and limbs chasing after a black and white ball churning up my playground. During the week it was a perfect carpet of field daisies that I had all to myself – just me and the *rumtumdawlies*.

While Ted might have been the star on the field, his light certainly didn't shine as brightly on the home front. Living right next door, Auntie Una and Uncle Koosie heard it all.

"Man, Jenny," Auntie Una recalled in her melodious timbre. "Your mum and dad used to fight a lot – especially on weekends."

In the midst of this squabbling and in-fighting, there were moments of comic relief even if it didn't seem so for them at the time. It was late one Saturday afternoon, Auntie Una told me, Ted had come home after soccer for a bath. As with most homes in our area with no indoor plumbing, bathing happened in the kitchen in a galvanized tub. Blackburns had

beaten St.Albans and Ted was in high spirits. He had plans to
go out and celebrate.

With two small children hanging onto her skirt the
whole day, it was easy to understand Ray being livid about
Ted's intentions. Through the thin row house dividing wall,
Aunt Una heard Ray's shrill voice protesting vehemently.

'I'm sick and tired of being left on my own every weekend.
You so damn inconsiderate! Here I am pregnant and you
don't care – you don't help out.'

'Hey, I go to work every day,' Ted shouted back, 'I provide
for you.   Must I sit at home every weekend holding your
hand? Why do you begrudge me playing soccer? Other wives
support their husbands. Why can't you? I'm their star player.'

'Star player! I'll give you a *blerrie* star.'

There was a crashing sound against the wall.

"*Jy's mal, man.* "I'm going!"

Peering through her window Auntie Una saw Ted, his
head shining with *Brylcreem,* walking briskly through the
broken gate across the field to the bus on Flinders Street, no
doubt on his way to raise a glass or two with the 'boys.'

In the small hours of the morning Auntie Una was
woken by Ted's banging on his front door asking Ray to
open up. All she could hear was Ted's repeated plea, 'Ray…
Ray… *maak oepie deur,*….Ray… Ray… *maak oepie deur,
man.*' Eventually he must have gone round to try the back
door because when she heard his voice again the sound was
muffled. Then came the cracking of breaking glass, followed
shortly by a loud thud and a lot of cursing. After that things
went quiet. It all came out later that day. Ted had inverted
the garbage bin under the kitchen window, grabbed a piece
of wood, climbed up and smashed the pane. Reaching in, he
had unlatched the window and hauled himself over the sill.
Being somewhat inebriated and unaware of the bathwater
left there from earlier in the evening, Ted got a rude shock
when he landed straight in the tub of cold water.

This was the first time I had heard this story and had to laugh at Auntie Una's humorous account. She always loved to tell a yarn especially when she had an appreciative audience in me.

"Oo, Jenny, there was always drama with your parents," she said as her giggles trailed off.

It was very much a man's world in South Africa. Men were able to pursue their passions while women were expected to keep house and raise the children. Here was Ray, not yet twenty five, pregnant with her fourth child. Her world was imploding. This all came to light when she visited me while I was living in New Zealand. We were at a café overlooking the Pacific Ocean enjoying one of the things they do so well down there, lattes and cappuccinos. The setting was in such contrast to what she had to say.

With no access to any family planning education or counseling, Coloured women took advice from their elders. And this often came down to old wives tales such as the more children a woman had, the healthier she would be. Children were also regarded as a natural extension of marriage and as I mentioned before, prospective future wage earners for the family. So, Ray had reluctantly resigned herself to getting pregnant year after year.

"Did you always want such a large family?" I asked.

"Heavens no! I just wanted maybe about two or three children."

She said she became exhausted and fell into severe depression and simply wanted to find a way out of her misery. The newspaper frequently reported incidents of people hurling themselves into the Brackenfell quarry. Ray decided that this was the way she'd end her life. She asked my cousin, Connie, to mind the children, and then cut across the field toward Flinders Street to wait for Mr. Burns' taxi. Mama saw her from the kitchen window and called out after her. She must have sensed from Ray's bearing that something was wrong.

"I had tears in my eyes, but I just told Mama I was all right and was going to the Mr. Ali's shop to buy bread or something. Mama tried to get me to come inside but I just walked away. I was waiting for Mr. Burns' taxi, when your dad came out of Mr. Ali's shop. He asked me where I was going. I just said, 'What do you care?' Man, Jennifer, I was so depressed, I just wanted to do away with myself. Shame, your dad still had a packet of doughnuts and snowballs (coconut cakes) he bought at Mr. Ali's."

"So what did he do?" I asked.

"He said, 'Hey, Ray – it's awright, man? It's okay. Let me take you home.'"

'I said I didn't want to go home. I hated my life and I couldn't take it anymore. I just want to go to the quarry and put an end to my life.'

"So did he talk you out of it?"

"Yes," she replied.

I could sense the awkwardness in her voice and demeanor.

"He said 'Ray, stop talking nonsense now. Come now, let me take you home.'"

"We stopped by Mama's place. She knew something was very wrong. Then she said to me, 'Ray don't you think it's time you gave your heart to the Lord? I knew Mama was right. Not long after that, George MacGregor held a tent meeting in Hamilton Street, next to the MacGregor's shop, you know?"

"Yes, I do. I remember they had a pigeon coop next to the shop."

"*Joh*, but you have a good memory, hey?" said Ray. "Anyway, I was at home and I could hear the wind carrying MacGregor's voice all the way from there. I could hear every word.

He was preaching the gospel and gave the invitation for people to come forward. Then a voice whispered in my ear – it was the Lord's voice, 'Come to me my child.' It was so clear, and I got up and started walking down the dark road to the tent. I knelt there in the sawdust and gave my heart to the Lord."

"How were things after that?"

By the look on her face it was clear that she was reliving that moment.

"I felt so calm and peaceful."

"And after that," her voice growing louder as she got excited, "Your dad, Lina and Danie, and all that crop of friends we used to party with, also got saved. Then we started living for the Lord. We went to church, prayer meetings and Bible studies. Our lives were peaceful from then onward. We used to go to the Mission, but then Pastor Valentine started a church in Windermere."

I well remember those tent meetings in Vasco, the only act in town, as it were. These were the days before television. George MacGregor and Andrew Valentine would pitch their circus-sized canvas tent on the open field next to the MacGregor clan's shops. During the day, someone would drive up and down the neighborhood, bullhorn in hand, "Come tonight, at seven o'clock to the tent on the field on Hamilton Street. Come hear God's anointed, A.J.J. Valentine! Bring your sick and downhearted and receive your miracle!" These crusade meetings as they called them occurred once a year or so, running from Sunday to Sunday.

At night the tent was aglow with a constellation of electric light bulbs powered by a noisy generator. The pine aroma of sawdust reminding me of the butcher's shop, permeated the air. Rows of low benches arranged in a semi-circle faced the raised stage. The pianist played peppy gospel tunes of the day as the crowd filed in packing out the place, while diminutive Sister Bessie squeezed her accordion enthusiastically, dwarfed by the large instrument. The tent reverberated with the sound of spirited happy-clappy singing.

'Pass along the invitation, pass along the word of God, until every tribe and nation shall have heard of Christ the Lord, Shall have heard… shall have heard, shall have heard of Christ the Lord," the choir sang. There would be praying, a word of welcome and more singing before some local "celebrity" gospel singer would step up to the microphone and do his thing. Hearty, appreciative 'amens' went up when he was done. From time to time, the microphone would screech, the animated announcer would blow into it a few times, and say, "Praise the Lord! Are you happy to be in the presence of the Lord?" and the congregation would answer with yet another hearty "Amen!"

"And now, without further ado, let me introduce God's anointed, Pastor A.J.J. Valentine!" Clambering over a tangle of amplifier wiring, Pastor Valentine, fiery preacher that he was, stepped up to the microphone. It was at just such a tent meeting, Ray and subsequently Ted, Lina and a group of their friends committed themselves to a life of piety and sobriety. It was a major turning point in my family's history.

After Ted's conversion, he had to give up any aspirations of soccer stardom. Pentecostalism demanded that personal ambitions be surrendered in order to devote life exclusively to the Lord's work. This also marked the time when he moved from blue to white collar work. He started work as a salesman for Singer Sewing Machines and then for Lewis Furniture Stores. Without the eight to five slog he now had more time for home life and church work as an elder. Saturdays were still his big days, now no longer soccer, but as a commission salesman he had to make his "collecting" rounds and Saturday was the best day to find his customers home.

Good customers had their installments duly set aside for him while others, when they saw his car, drew their curtains and locked their doors, pretending to be out. He told of one negligent customer, when he arrived at her house, her small child answered the door saying "My mummy says to tell Mr. Paulse, my mummy went out." Ted saw the mummy's feet sticking out from under the drawn curtain. "Tell your mummy," Ted replied, "Next time she goes out, she must take her feet with her."

Somewhere along the way, I remember a brouhaha between my father and Pastor Valentine over church politics. Things became acrimonious forcing Ted to leave. He felt God's calling him to step up to leadership and go into full-time ministry. He was burdened to do something to spiritually alleviate the lot of those on the Cape Flats. On weekends when drinking and *dagga*-smoking proliferated, stabbings and rape were the order of the day, Ted gathered a group of Christians together for prayer meetings and Bible study and before long, he had established a congregation numbering in the hundreds.

In those days, in South Africa, the Pentecostal church had no seminaries for pastors that I knew of. Consequently, some of the teachings disseminated from the pulpit were repressive and legalistic. A number of Coloured Pentecostal preachers had the attitude that seminaries weren't important as all they needed was the Holy Spirit.

Sadly, the care Ted lavished on his Sherwood Park *Assembly of God* congregation, wasn't mirrored in our home. God's "work" took precedence over his family (something he regretted toward the end of his life.) He practiced parenting skills (or lack thereof) he had learned from his parents and societal norms of the time.

When it came to his family he wasn't demonstrative. In fairness to him, he probably didn't know how. My youngest brother, David, relates when he was about seven years old he was over at his playmate, Aziz's house. The boys were playing on the *stoep* when Aziz's father stepped out the door. Aziz ran to his dad and playfully started boxing him. His father responded in kind wrestling him to the ground, tickling the boy and tousling his hair. Aziz's giggles gave way to loud peals of laughter.

David remarked he longed to have that kind of relationship with our dad. When he went home, he ran to Ted and playfully punched him in the belly.

"Hey!" Ted cried. Whether he was taken aback, or uncertain as to how to respond is unclear, but he reacted with, "What do you think you're doing?"

His short, muscular arms flailed clumsily, in the process cuffing my brother's skinny frame. To some extent, David understood that it was not a beating - more that Ted was taken by surprise. It was not the sting of the blows that hurt, the pain went much deeper – it was the disappointment of Ted not being able to demonstrate any affection or tenderness toward his son. David said his bottom lip began to quiver and he ran to his room sobbing. "Now what?" Ted said irritably and perplexed."What's your problem? What are you crying about?"

Chapter 11

Carnival Time

We peeled our eyes for Uncle Albert. He didn't play an instrument, he just marched.

"There he is!" someone shouted.

"Albert!" we cheered, "Uncle Albert!" trying vainly to be heard above the din of the music.

Uncle Albert, resplendent in the band's uniform of navy blazer, white slacks, smart tie, topped with Panama hat, swung his arms ramrod straight, not looking to the left or the right.

It was late afternoon, on Christmas day. Our appetites were satiated and our stomachs distended. We could hear Christmas carols carried on the breeze throughout the neighborhood. As the sound drew nearer, we gathered by the roadside - Mama, Papa, aunts, uncles, cousins and neighbours. We knew Uncle Albert's troupe would be passing by our house. The fancy banner emblazoned with the band's name was now clearly in view. In the forefront the drum major deftly waved and twirled his mace. The *ghoema* beat, "Choom-chicka-choom-chicka choom" rendition of "Hark the Herald Angels Sing" on guitars, trumpets, saxophones and banjo now drowned out our cheering. The Christmas bands were the prelude to the annual Cape Town Coon Carnival.

In my community the week between Christmas and New Year was known as 'The Big Days.'

This was when all sorts of cultural and community activities took place. December and January being the middle of summer in the southern hemisphere, was when most people took their vacation. Schools were out and factories closed between mid-December and mid-January.

During this time "lay buys" on new clothes, linen and housewares, paid for in instalments during the year, would be procured. The Coloureds adopted the "turning out" tradition possibly from the Malay culture of doing a thorough house spring-cleaning leading up to the "Big Days." This meant painting the house, getting new curtains, mats, linen and bedding and so forth. This was the time when housewives showed their prowess in the kitchen turning out delicious fruitcakes, tarts, preserves and wonderful holiday fare. It was a time of plenty that came once a year when we could feast to our heart's content.

On Christmas evening we joined the throng downtown to see the glittering Christmas lights and decorations. A festive air permeated the teeming sidewalks with intermittent jolly toot-toot-toots resounding from cars crawling on Adderley Street. All eyes gazed in wonderment at the animated display of Father Christmas (Santa) and his reindeer up above the cantilevered façade of one of departmental stores depicting a northern hemisphere winter scene. I was simply awestruck by the moving figures. This, together with candle and bow shaped lights and the like made Christmas all the more magical.

In and around the Christmas and New Year period was carnival time in Cape Town, a tradition founded on a custom dating back to 17th century slavery times. Cape slaves were given one day off every year on which they could let their hair down and indulge in jollification. That day, unique to Cape Town, fell on January 2, known as *Tweede Nuwe Jaar*,

This custom started out as unorganized revelry giving root in later years to what we knew as The Cape Town Coon

Carnival (Today, The Cape Town Minstrels.) Unlike the derogatory connotation the word "coon" conveys in the United States, in South Africa it was simply connected to the art and festivities of the performing minstrels, strangely devoid of any racial slur.

Coons were also known as *klopse*, especially among the Brown people. *Klopse, Nagtroepe* (Malay choirs) and Christmas bands performed under different genre. While the *nagtroepe* sang songs derived from Dutch folk, *moppies* (comic songs) and pop songs of the day, Christmas bands performed traditional carols and hymns. But it was the *klopse* that attracted the crowds.

As a young girl, every *Tweede Nuwe Jaar*, I went downtown with my family to see the *klopse*. These minstrels decked out in a colour-burst of satin costumes, jitterbugged down Adderley Street, twirling brightly striped umbrellas above their heads. Capetonians, mainly Coloureds and Whites spilled into the city centre, full of bonhomie, wishing and kissing each other "Happy New Year," revelling in the colourful display of *klopse* performing ribald songs and dance routines. The way we all intermingled, you'd have thought that apartheid had taken a day off.

Carnival preparations began months in advance at the homes of troupe leaders where troupes with curious names like *The Pennsylvannias, The Apaches* and *The Atjas*, designed their costumes and practiced their song and dance routines. It was the *Atjas* who struck fear in the hearts of all children. Inspired by American Red Indians, *Atjas,* (also known to us kids as the *Atja Americans*) donned feathered headgears, scary masks or war-painted faces. Brandishing fake tomahawks, the performers would break away from their troupe and give chase to hapless kids, threatening to scalp them.

True to form all this revelry between the Whites and Coloureds was too much for the government. They were concerned about the influx of masses of Non-White people in the downtown area, and bothered about the camaraderie between the races. Systematically they began to bring down the curtain on the Carnival. In 1967, they banned troupes from performing at Green Point Stadium. The following year they put an end to the Coons parading in Cape Town city centre. From 1971, Athlone Stadium was used for Non-White spectators. During the 1970s, traffic bylaws and the "Illegal Gathering Act" were used to place further difficulties on the minstrel organizers. It was a sad time for all Capetonians as the Carnival had been such an integral part of Cape Town.

Chapter 12

Lion To Lamb

Papa was as predictable as a clock – well, that's the Papa I always knew. I can still see it so clearly today, Papa's Studebaker trundling down the dirt driveway at six o' clock and coming to a halt just outside the kitchen door. With his small wooden case in hand Papa would walk straight to Mama busy at the stove. I knew exactly what he was going to say. "Hello *Bokkie*," and then he'd plant three kisses on her mouth. The two of them would then glance at me and laugh as I looked on grinning. The fragrant aroma of *Koffiehuis* brewing in the percolator on the stove, mingling with whatever delicious fare was baking in the oven, permeated the kitchen. Mama would then pour Papa his usual cup of coffee.

Over supper at the kitchen table, Papa would regale us with stories of his day at Oros Lemos where he worked as a maintenance engineer. Sometimes, tears rolled down his eyes when he told of Pung's shenanigans. All I know is that Pung was a character at work. I would laugh because of Papa's cackling, even when I didn't necessarily know what was so funny.

Routinely, on Saturday evenings Papa would gather up our Sunday-best shoes, have the *Kiwi* polish and brush in hand, he'd set himself up at the kitchen table by the bright glow of the Tilly lamp. Job done, with shoes spit spot ready for The Lord's Day, he'd bring out the weekend *Argus* which he'd proceed to read from cover to cover, always leaving the obituary column for last. Sometimes I'd stand behind him playing with his hair. He didn't seem to mind, in fact, I'm sure he really enjoyed it. I liked to practice braiding on him but somehow the braid ended sticking straight up like a small chimney.

"Oh Tom, you should see yourself!" Mama laughed.

Papa would look at me with amusement and his face would break into a gapped-tooth grin.

Every so often on a sunny Sunday afternoon, Papa would take us for a, "joy ride" into the country. Mama and I would sing merrily while Papa whistled along.

Sometimes Papa would get it into his head to go look up long lost relatives. Not my favourite pastime.

It was always a hit and miss mission. None of us had phones in those days. So whether we'd find our kin at home or even find them at all was anyone's guess. It would always follow the same rigmarole.

We'd breeze into some small *dorp*, stopping when he spotted someone walking along the roadside.

"*Boytjie*," he'd say, "Do you know where so-and-so lives?" Invariably the boy would scratch his head.

"*Nee meneer*," he'd reply, his face completely blank. Papa would then drive on slowly till he saw another person.

This is exactly the way it was when we visited the Cloetes. The first boytjie had no idea, but we got lucky on our second stop.

"Hallo, do you perhaps know where the Cloetes lives?"

"Cloetes? ... Cloetes?" replied the man, looking up at the sky as if for help.

'Ja, Pieter Cloete," Papa said searching the shriveled face.

"Oooe, Piet Cloete!" A light seemed to turn on in his brain. "*Meneer* passed the turn to Piet's place, he said in Afrikaans. After a long pause, he pointed back, saying "*Meneer* must turn around, drive through the dorp till *meneer* comes to the Caltex Garage...then *meneer* must take..."

"*Ja, ja, ja,*" was Papa's intermittent rejoinder, taking in the man's long-winded directions. It took us several attempts to finally find Piet Cloete's white-washed farm-workers' cottage. We spilled out of the car, making our way to the stable style door. "Hallo?" Papa called. We waited. "Hallo?"

"A bleary eyed figure finally appeared at the door," squinting into the blinding sunlight.

"We're looking for Piet Cloete," Papa said. Mama smiled brightly while I apprehensively surveyed the darkness beyond the door wishing that we didn't have to go into the cottage.

"*Ek is Piet Cloete,*" the man replied with a look of perplexity. It was clearly evident he'd been disturbed from his afternoon nap. Papa explained who he was, the cousin of so and so, three times removed. After Piet Cloete connected the dots he said, "*Kom binne.*"

We entered the dingy cottage and sat in the humble living room-cum-kitchen while Piet Cloete disappeared to summon his wife. With introductions done, Mrs. Cloete lit the Primus stove to get the kettle going. Conversation between the long-lost relatives came in fits and starts. Piet and his wife looked very much like they'd rather still be sleeping. I was bored silly. Mrs. Cloete went outside to call some children to play with me. I really just wanted to go home. These *plaas* people were just too different for a little city slicker like me.

And to crown it all, on our way back from these country jaunts, Papa would invariably stop to pick up hitchhiking farm workers along the road. More often than not, they'd be inebriated, and when they piled into the back seat they'd breathe boozy fumes all over me. Papa picked them up to share the Gospel. Gospel or not, I didn't like these *dronkies* ruining my joy ride.

But Papa was not always this caring and magnanimous. He had a notorious past. Growing up, I heard snippets of his legendary temper and his "Lion to Lamb" conversion. As a child I regarded this story as some kind of Grimms Brothers fairytale because I'd known only Papa's "lamb" side. It was at one of George Macgregor's tent meetings that Mama went forward and committed her life to the Lord. From that time on her burning desire was to get Papa "saved." She prayed regularly with her friend Nellie Macgregor, George's aunt that Papa would turn from his transgressions.

The turning point in Papa's life came in dramatic fashion. From all accounts, the news of his "conversion" spread through the neighborhood like wildfire and it wasn't long before everyone was party to the details of how it all came about. I was a toddler at the time, oblivious to all these happenings let alone the magnitude of the changes taking place.

"Agh Jenny," Auntie Una began. Even in recounting such an unpleasant episode of our family history, her voice maintained its natural melodic quality.

"Man, Jenny," she continued, "Uncle Koosie and I were in a deep sleep, when we heard loud banging on our door. I looked out the window and there was Mama and Albe in their nighties with Mr. and Mrs. Johnson."

Mr. Johnson said Papa was in one of his moods again and had threatened to kill Mama.

"Jennifer, with all the noise going on outside, your mum came out too. Poor Mama was in such a state, she just collapsed into my arms, man. And poor Albe was so pale, standing there with her hands over her face just weeping.

Jenny, Mama cried out to God, 'I can't live like this anymore, do something with Tom! Oh God, either take him or take me, but I can't go on like this…'"

It was obviously a tumultuous night by all accounts, but it was far from over.

"Jennifer," Auntie Una paused briefly. "Early the next morning, there was again a banging on the door. This time it was Papa. Oh, he was in a terrible state, man. He was sobbing, 'Oh God Una, I killed your mother.'

I told him, "No Daddy, you *almost* killed her. If it wasn't for Albe, Mummy *would* be dead."

He said to me, 'I'm sorry, I'm so sorry."

It took a while for him to register what Auntie Una had said before he asked,

'Where's your mother now, Una?'

Auntie Una said she wouldn't tell him.

By this time Ray, who had gone back to her house earlier, had come across from next door barging past Papa standing on the doorstep.

"Jenny, we all didn't sleep that night and Ray was so cross, man. She really told him off. She said 'Enough is enough, you mad and don't come here with your crocodile tears.'

Where I plucked up the courage to say what I said to Papa, I don't know, but this is what I told him. 'Daddy, this had to be said a long time ago, and I'm going to say it now. You are a sorry excuse for a man and a father. You should be ashamed of yourself for the way you've treated our mother all these years. You have snuffed out the joy and beauty out of a good person. You keep terrorizing her and then you just say "sorry" every time. Why Mummy hasn't left you a long time ago, I'll never know. May God deal with you for your cruelty."

Auntie Una's eyes softened as she said,

"Jenny, then Papa said to me, 'Una, hear me out. You must believe me. God *did* deal with me!'

Your mum chimed in asking him what he was talking about and told him that he was still drunk.

Papa said, '*Nee, my kind*, I've never been more sober. God got hold of me during the night.

I must ask your mother's forgiveness. Where is she? Please tell me.'"

Auntie Una said they had never seen him so remorseful and could see he was genuine and they believed him. Auntie Una, clearly taking pleasure in relating the story was more than forthcoming.

"Papa said, 'Where is your mother? I swear to God I'll do her no harm. I want to make peace with her and with God. Please Una, I beg you, let me see her so I can ask forgiveness.'"

By now, according to Auntie Una, Mama, who had heard the conversation, came to the door.

Papa's sobs intensified when he saw her. "Man, I couldn't help feeling sorry for him. He was crying so much when he said, 'Margaret, something happened to me last night. God spoke to me in a dream...'" He explained what he had experienced. He'd had a nightmare and there was blood everywhere. Mama lay on the bed dead, her eyes still open but very sad. Then her face morphed into that of Jesus' whose eyes were full of compassion. He said he knew this was his day of salvation and that he cried out to God for forgiveness.

"Jenny, Papa said to Mama, 'Margaret, now I'm asking you to please forgive me.'"

During the course of the next few days, the whole saga of Papa's conversion unfolded. That night, Papa staggered home from one of his drinking binges apparently shouting obscenities and oaths at no one in particular. He stormed into the bedroom, waking Mama up, shouting expletives at her. Wild-eyed, he suddenly lifted the double bed with Mama in it and turned it upside down. Mama pleaded with him to stop, but he kept swearing at her and saying he was going to get his axe to kill her.

With Papa stumbling around in the dark outside, Albe who had heard the commotion, came flying into the bedroom and dragged Mama out from under the upturned bed. Clad only in their nightdresses, the two women fled out through the front door across the road to the Johnson's house. Being no stranger to Papa's violent outbursts, Mr. Johnson knew he needed to take them to a place of safety and escorted them across the field to Auntie Una's.

Meanwhile Papa had apparently collapsed on his bed which he somehow must have turned right side up. He had some kind of nightmare or hallucination. When he woke up, and saw Mama was not in the bed next to him, he was convinced that he had killed her.

He rushed out the front door making his way to the large daisy bush near the street looking for her body, no doubt frantic with guilt, remorse and fear. That's when Una found him on her doorstep and he found out Mama was alive.

I have no recollection of such goings-on. Where I was in all this, no one can tell me, but I was blissfully unaware of such horrific scenes and I'm glad that I knew only the "lamb" part of Papa.

Chapter 13

Sundays

"Pentecost is real, no matter what they say, Pentecost is real, I'm on the narrow way, Pentecost is real, By the Spirit say, Hallelujah, Praise the Lord, I know, I know it's real.

Pentecost is real, no matter what they say, Pentecost is........." on and on the opening chorus would be sung accompanied by guitar and accordion and spirited handclapping. And just when you thought it was over one of the 'brothers' up front would jump in with another chorus.

I was about three years old when we started going to church, so my lasting memory of Sundays was always associated with church. I was told I was christened at St Alban's Anglican Church and how long we attended on a regular basis I don't know. But I have total recall when it comes to the fetes in the church hall. The stalls set out in the musty old church hall were laden with bric-'n-brac, used clothing, and baked goodies. I would always make a beeline to the Easter baskets. I loved the way those handmade cardboard baskets were put together and decorated with colourful cellophane and pastel straw. I couldn't wait to see what was inside - Easter eggs, candies and monkey nuts. We kids would jabber excitedly among each other as we compared the contents of our baskets.

"What did you get?"

"Oh look, you got a whistle…"

Sunday was like no other day of the week. Everyday activities stopped. Merchants throughout the land closed their stores. Everyone went to church. Well at least that's the way it seemed to me when I was growing up. In our community, preparation for church began with a Saturday evening bath ritual. We had no bathrooms. So, the large galvanized tub that was also used for laundry was brought into the kitchen where we used the hot water from the boiler attached to the wood burning stove. Pales of water were carried in from the free-standing outside tap to keep the boiler topped up. This was our only source of water. The 'bonus' of bathing in the kitchen in winter was benefiting from the warmth of the stove when getting out of the tub. There was a sequence to bath time – children first, then the adults. We all used the same water. The tub would be emptied the next morning scooping the water out bucket by bucket and ditching it on the grass outside. Children, when old enough, became the bucket brigade. When sufficiently empty, one of the grown-ups would drag the tub through the back door and pour out the remaining water. For the rest of the week we performed our ablutions 'cowboy style.' We had a blue enamel pitcher and basin for this purpose.

You dressed up for church in those days. I don't know how it made others feel, but I always felt proud as a peacock in my taffeta dress with satin bows that Mama had made for me. Although I didn't like the thin elastic attached at the sides of my hat that cut under my chin, it served as a useful distraction to chew on when bored during the sermon. Mama would usually nudge me and shake her head in disapproval.

By the time I was five years old we were going to the City Mission on Riebeeck Street. It was a lot closer to home, right across the field. The Mission was a plain white-washed Moorish-style building complete with gable and bell. I can still hear its tinny sound calling the faithful to worship. The wooden pews were uncushioned, the air was musty and there would be Mrs. Wastey belting out hymns on the old organ wheezing away like someone with bad asthma. Many from our neighbourhood including my family were adherents there but I always sat with Mama.

Mama was well known and respected for her good works in the community, sewing for the poor, baking for social events and singing at church socials. My mother's lasting recollection of the City Mission was the time she went with Mama to a social where Mama was the soloist.

There they were all pressed out for occasion. But I can just picture Mama in a black chiffon, belted dress demurely holding her satin-gloved hands together warbling away in her Gracie Fields voice.

"Do you remember Mr Eckard?" Ray asked.

I shook my head from side to side.

"Man, Mr. Eckard used to play the violin for Mama".

"*Hy was so 'n klein mannetjie*", she chuckled, clearly seeing him in her mind's eye after all those years. Ray lapsed between English and Afrikaans in the typical way of most Coloured people.

"Man, after Mama finished, he took Mama's hand and walked her down from the stage to come sit by us. "You sang very nice," Mr. Eckard said.

Later, after tea and cake, Mr Eckard, offered to walk the two of them home across the inky field. As they approached the house, they could see Papa standing in the doorway, his figure silhouetted against light cast by the Tilly lamp in the kitchen.

"Man, when we got to the back door," Ray began to titter. "Mr Eckard said, 'Good evening Mr. Whitman, Mrs. Whitman did you pro…'" By now Ray was having a hard time containing her laughter.

"There Papa grabbed the violin case out of Mr. Eckard's hand, and shame, before he could finish the word "proud," Papa hit him on the head *met die verjooltjie*." I couldn't help laughing with Ray at this comedic sight.

"*Ai*, that man, hey?" Ray shook her head from side to side, still laughing.

"Was it just jealousy or had he been drinking?" I asked after Ray gained her composure.

"*Ja*, it was probably both," she replied.

"What happened to Mr Eckard?"

"Shame, he just grabbed his violin and ran like mad."

"What did you and Mama do?"

"He shouted at us to get inside and we both ran inside, 'cause when Papa was like that, Lord help us."

Sunday wasn't Sunday without the traditional roast. This was very much a countrywide custom, churchgoer or not. Arriving home we would be greeted by the tantalizing aroma of roast meat and potatoes that Mama had put in the oven before leaving. Papa would switch on the transistor radio and turn the dial amid much static screeching till he found Springbok radio. At twelve o' clock, Simon Swindell's smooth voice would announce, "From the Bell Tower," a program synonymous with Sundays, followed by a salvo of sacred tunes. Songsters such as The Mormon Tabernacle Choir, George Beverley Shea, Jim Reeves and Slim Whitman were favourites. Mama would warble along with them as she prepared lunch.

My job was to help Auntie Albe set the table. We always ate in the kitchen. It was only on very special occasions, weddings, birthday parties, Christmas that we would use the dining room table that stood in the 'voorkamer'. Then the white linen tablecloth, the plated silver cutlery, and china ware would all come out of the sideboard. Forks on the left of the plates, bone-handled knives on the right, and the dessertspoons at the twelve o'clock position, Auntie Albe would gently instruct me in her inimitable quiet manner. The food would be blessed and then we would tuck into to the sumptuous fare - roast beef or lamb with gravy, golden crispy potatoes, carrots, peas and beetroot salad followed by Mama's home-preserved guavas topped with smooth, yellow custard.

Sunday was literally a day of rest. Nothing stirred, at least not inside where the grownups were taking a nap. But we children always found something to do. But it had to happen outside. It was tantamount to sin to disturb the indoor peace and quiet. Mama's yard was a wonderful place for endless games. I can still remember the playground song we sang when we played skipping rope:

Ten o'clock is striking, my ma won't let me out
My young man is waiting; he wants to take me out
He takes me round the corner; he takes me over the sea
He takes me to my uncle to have a cup of tea
A stands for apple, B stands for bell
And C stands for Cecil and Cecil's gone to hell.

Sometimes we played on the field calling up the rumtumdawlies. For this you needed a straight twig and an old tin can. You stuck the twig into a soft grassy patch and chanted, "Rumtumdawly, Chip Chap Charlie, *Ooe, jou huisie brand uit.*" (Rumtumdawly, Chip Chap Charlie, ooh, your house is on fire) all the while rotating the stick. You kept your eyes peeled for the earthworms desperately squirming out of the ground because of the vibration, then you'd bag them in your tin. Like hunters boasting over their spoils, we would compare our wriggly finds. The mothers would scold us with a 'Oh sis man! Messing with worms. Go wash your hands and get ready for Sunday school!'

There we'd sing our hearts out, "A sunbeam, a sunbeam, Jesus wants me for a sunbeam...I'll be a sunbeam for him." Mr. Lawrence's mesmerizing green eyes, kept our attention as he told us Bible stories. Mama always tied a penny in the corner of my handkerchief for collection. As the velvet collection bag was being passed along the pews, we'd all sing heartily, "Hear the pennies dropping, listen how they fall, everyone for Jesus, he will bless them all. Dropping, dropping, dropping, dropping, hear the pennies fall, everyone for Jesus, he will bless them all." But the best part of Sunday school was being blessed with a biscuit or candy afterward.

Our time at the City Mission was short-lived. The family started attending Pastor Valentine's church as he had been instrumental in their conversion to Pentacostalism. When I say Pastor Valentine's church, it was actually a dingy community hall - a dank building with high windows, situated between rows of scruffy, crowded houses. I hated that place. In my mind this was not 'proper' church, like St. Albans and the City Mission. To get to the door we had to negotiate our way over a makeshift paving slab that bridged a dirty, slimy, open ditch. During the rainy season the detritus flowed, but on a hot day, it lay stagnant, stinking to high heaven. Invariably one of us kids would accidently step in the muck, soiling her best white socks.

Andrew J. Valentine, trained as a primary school teacher, heard God's "calling" and collaborated with George Macgregor in "harvesting" the spiritual fields of Vasco. Pastor Valentines' church was very different from the City Mission. There was no liturgy and formal order of service, to me the whole thing seemed too much like a free-for-all: congregants raising their hands, some sobbing, some clapping, some speaking in tongues and the constant interjection of amens and hallelujahs. And the services went on forever and ever.

A lean, swarthy man, Pastor Valentine was an animated orator. He could certainly keep an audience captivated. He clearly styled himself after American evangelists of the day. Sometimes when the Spirit really moved him, he spoke so fervently that his gold tooth popped out, sabotaging his speech. Without missing a beat, he'd pop it right back in place to drive his point home. He would pause, his fiery gaze scanning the congregation as he waited for an "amen."

To illustrate a point, he often used a member of the congregation as an example.

"Brothers and sisters, the Bible says that if Jesus sets you free, you are free, indeed!"

"Amen!" the church would chorus.

"He set Brother Whitman free in Vasco," Pastor Valentine pointed to Papa in our row.

"He turned Brother Whitman from a lion into a lamb, Brothers and Sisters!"

"Amen! Hallelujah! Glory to God!" Pastor Valentine's pink lizard tongue had a way of shooting out over his upper lip a lot when he was on a roll.

"Here was a man, Brothers and Sisters, that was so bound by the chains of Satan, that when his wife was on her knees praying for him, he pulled her up by her plaits, and shouted, 'You get your God down here in front of me so I can see him, then I'll believe."

"But glory to God!" Pastor Valentine continued, his face shiny with perspiration,

"The Son of God set him free!"

"Amen," Mama chorused along with others. I looked up at Papa and saw his eyes tearing up.

Years later, when the church's venue changed to SHAWCO's health and welfare facilities in Kensington, Pastor Valentine embarked on a building program. But first he needed to go to America to raise funds. Gone for a number of months, he returned with not only his usual fervor but now speaking with an American twang. To us, he was like Moses who had been on the mountain top. He had been to America, the Promised Land. His sermons were now peppered with name-dropping. "When I was in Detroit City," he would wax forth..." Just the name of the place gave me the impression that this was some place really special.

Little did I know that it was Motown from where my favorite musicians came.

Years went by and no building materialized. The choir had a number they used to sing, "Give of your best to the Master," but one disgruntled member wondering where the tithes and building funds were going, declared huffily, "It's not 'Give of Your Best to the Master,' it's more like 'Give of Your Best to Your Pastor!'"

Chapter 14

The Living Sound

Evangelistic tent meetings, American style, were popular events of the day. In the Coloured community we didn't have a whole lot going on. So when one of the itinerant preachers pitched his tent, you could be sure of a good turnout. On the occasions an American preacher came into town, people would come in droves. And when he made an altar call, the crowds would swarm to the front without needing much coercion. Some with bowed heads and others openly crying, they'd jostle to get a good spot so they could be touched by the white preacher. The Mixed-Race people for the most part could be naïve and gullible and anything that came out of America we thought magical.

One time a Christian contemporary band and singing group from the Oral Roberts University of Tulsa, Oklahoma breezed into Cape Town, performing at Athlone Stadium and to a mixed audience in Cape Town City Hall. Our minister Pastor Valentine, having connections with the groups' promoter was able to get *The Living Sound* to hold meetings in our area. When the team accepted Auntie Una's invitation for supper the women in my family, sprang into action, cleaning house, rearranging furniture and making a *lang tafel* to put on an unforgettable meal of traditional Capetonian food. When we kids heard *The Living Sound* was coming to Auntie Una's house we could hardly contain ourselves.

We jammed our faces up against the window pane. Every time car lights approached one of us would shout out, "Here they come! Here they come!"

When the car passed by, we gave a collective groan. "No man, they coming in a van!" someone else would say.

Uncle Koosie, looking at his watch, not for the first time, muttered that they were supposed to be there at nine o'clock and it was almost ten. "Where are these people then, man?"

"I suppose they're packing up their equipment and everything," Auntie Una replied, reaching out to straighten the flower arrangement on the buffet table for the umpteenth time.

"Tsk, now the food is getting cold, man," Ray grumbled.

"They coming, they coming…They here!" screamed a cousin, holding the living room curtains apart, his eyes like saucers.

"You kids stand back!" Uncle Koosie scolded, as he backed us up in a pile into the hallway off the living room. We had memorized the singers' names when they were introduced at the concert.

"That's Jan!" one of the cousins whispered, as a dozen heads craned their necks round the door.

"No, it's not! It's Debbie!" I put forth, clearly in awe of the gorgeous American blue-eyed, beauty.

One by one they appeared through Auntie Una's front door, chatting in their inimitable drawl. They were blonde haired, red-haired, pink skinned. They were beautiful people like the Hollywood stars we saw on the screen at the bioscope.

We stood there mesmerized at what was taking place in Auntie Una's living room. We watched the fresh-faced young people's every move – the way they tucked into the food, their laughter, their sparkling blue eyes.

"Shame," someone remarked, for want of something to say.

"Look," my cousin poked me, "Ron put the whole savory tart in his mouth in one bite!"

We tittered. When one of the vocalists, Bev, came over to ask us where the toilet was, we were so star struck - I thought I was going to faint. A couple of us pointed down the hall and I shyly said, "There." Bev smelled as gorgeous as she looked and I thought, *Wow, this is the wonderful smell of America.*

After she used the loo, all of us suddenly wanted to go too, like the commode had somehow been transformed into The Holy Grail. For weeks to come all we would talk about was *The Living Sound.* And on Sunday, when Simon Swindoll played a *Living Sound* number on Springbok Radio's *From the Bell Tower*, we could all say, "We know them. They came to our house. We met them face to face. We shook their hands."

Chapter 15

Auntie Albe

Albertha Whitman, Auntie Albe to us kids, was the epitome of goodness. Reserved by nature, according to Ray and Una, she kept innermost feelings to herself seldom confiding in her older sisters. She loved whiling away a Saturday afternoon sunning herself in the yard when her chores were all done, letting the warm air dry her rolled hair as she pored over a magazine. She carried an air of calm and serenity about her.

I can still picture her in her flared gingham skirt, dainty white blouse and *Fair Isle* cardigan riding her bicycle to and from Poppies, the knitwear factory where she worked. She was fair skinned with dark hair she neatly tied on her nape with a ribbon matching her skirt. Her eyes were gentle and her dazzling smile revealed straight white teeth. She was a real Samaritan. One who if she saw someone laden with heavy grocery bags would stop her bike and lend a helping hand. Nobody had a bad word to say about Auntie Albe.

When I went with Auntie Albe on errands for Mama, I would ride on the carrier seat of her bicycle, splaying my legs so my feet wouldn't get caught in the spokes. Mrs. Prodgers' corner shop had a tin-roofed veranda that wrapped around part way around the building, providing shade from the hot summer sun. It didn't smell of curry, like Mr. Ali or Tanjeera's shops. Hers was always spotless with a wonderful aroma of fresh baked bread. I loved the homey feel of that shop - racks of neatly stacked canned and bottled groceries on the walls and of course those jars of candies set out on the solid wooden counter top.

I was often tempted to plunge my hands into the open burlap sacks on the floor filled with rice, dried beans and pulses but I knew better because my hand would get a swift smack. Mrs. Prodgers was White, English speaking and on friendly terms with the local housewives. At this point our area had not yet been declared White. Coloureds and Whites still lived side by side. Mrs. Prodgers was always clued up on all the *skinner* - who had what malady, who had just died, who had to have a 'must marriage' and who was *jolling* with whom.

She always gave us a welcoming smile peering through her gold-rimmed granny glasses. She had that classic Norman Rockwell look - wrinkled face with white hair in a bun. Anytime Mama wanted baloney I would watch with fascination as Mrs. Prodgers fed the red encased baloney roll through the electric meat slicer. I marveled how she managed not to cut her fingers.

And oh, those jars of wonderful assorted mouthwatering candies. They drew my covetous eyes like a magnet - Bulls Eyes, Stars that turned your teeth and tongue bright pink, Liquorice All Sorts, coils of Liquorice Drop, Sugas, Sherbet in parchment packets with Liquorice straws, Jelly Babies, necklaces of candies on a string, and my all-time favourite, well another one of my all-time favourites, Sweetie Pies wrapped in alluring red and gold foil.

Auntie Albe knew my weakness. She would invariably add a Sweetie Pie to the order. And I would always say the same thing, 'Thank you Auntie Albe!' And when Mrs Prodgers leaned over the counter to hand me the coveted confectionary, I would have a big 'thank you' for her too. That Sweetie Pie would be out of its wrapper and into my mouth before we ever got out of the door! How I loved that auntie! That memory is deliciously seared into my mind.

And then there was *pesella* – that little something extra.
Mrs. Prodgers would give me a reward for no particular
reason; maybe two Bulls Eyes or a few Stars. "Put that away
for tomorrow, dearie," she would say, "You'll get tummy ache
if you eat too many sweets at once."

Mama instilled in me never to ask for *pesella*, because
it was bad manners. I had witnessed cheeky children blurt
out, 'Half a pound of peanut butter and pesella, please Mrs
Prodgers. To which she would respond curtly, 'No *pesella*
today.' *Bonsella* was an Afrikaans corruption of the Zulu
word, *bansela* – giving of a small gift. But we had further
distorted the word to *pesella*.

In the summer of 1960, Auntie Albe got engaged to
Gert Wentzel. Nobody ever called him Gert. He was always
Wentzel or Brother Wentzel to the church people. I called
him Uncle Wentzel. Albe and Wentzel were your *Colgate*
couple; he tall, square-jawed, a gentleman of impeccable
manners, she sweet, demure with that radiant smile. Wentzel
drove an ancient Model T Ford. You had to crank the handle
in the front to get the engine started. Today it would be a
highly prized and priced collector's car. In those days it was a
bargain basement sort of vehicle.

I went with Albe and Wentzel one Sunday afternoon
when he was teaching her to drive. The back seat was so low,
or maybe I was just so small, that all I could see were tops
of trees, blue sky and electric power lines flying by. The best
part was Albe making the car jerk every time she let out the
clutch too soon. Not once did Wentzel raise his voice at her.
He was patience personified. But as with most lovers, they
had something of a tiff one evening. Albe retreated to her
bedroom leaving Wentzel to sit all forlorn in the *voorkamer*.
By the lamplight at the dining room table, he wrote on a
piece of paper, folded it and asked me to deliver it to Albe. I
took her the note and waited while she read it. She wrote a

reply and gave it to me to take back to him. I quite liked this 'game' of taking notes to and fro.

Wentzel was the future son-in-law every parent dreamed of. He would fulfil Mama's long-cherished 'white wedding' desire, and she would go to the Grand Parade, buy the best fabric she could afford, and pour her heart and soul into its construction of a wedding gown.

The day was cold and wet. Albe came cycling down the dirt driveway, soaked to the skin, looking pale and exhausted. Mama spotted her through the kitchen window, met her at the door and scolded her for not taking a raincoat, reminding her, as mothers did, that you always take a raincoat with you "just in case."

Some weeks later, Albe became listless, she couldn't go to work. The doctor found lumps under her armpits. In those days, doctors were revered. They would pronounce their diagnosis in medical parlance. We would never ask for an explanation or any details as to what exactly was wrong. Just as you never questioned the preacher's elucidation of a passage of Scripture, so you didn't ask a doctor to explain himself, a sad reality of what a lack of education can produce. Words like lymph nodes, diabetes or emotional disorder were terms not in our vocabulary. They'd simply be 'glands' or 'sugar' or 'nerves'. And the stock response would be, 'shame'.

Albe was suffering from 'glands' for which she was hospitalized. Mama, Papa and I padded down a long, gleaming corridor in Groote Schuur Hospital. We talked in hushed tones as if on hallowed ground. Mama commented on how pale Albe looked but she still managed her beautiful smile when she saw us. It was just not in her nature to complain. She weakly pulled the blanket down to show us her swollen legs and ankles. The doctors diagnosed her with pleurisy and double pneumonia. In retrospect we know now that these are related symptoms of cancer. If the doctors knew she had cancer, they certainly didn't inform any of us.

This was the first time I had been to a hospital. Patients in their beds, medical paraphernalia attached to walls and hanging from ceilings, nurses in starch uniforms bustling back and forth on squeaky shoes through swinging doors were all novel to me. While I knew something was wrong with my Auntie, as a typical five-year-old I was far more interested in all these new things around me and it wasn't long before my eyes settled on the candies next to the fruit and flowers on the bedside table. When she saw me eying them she offered them to me. How could a small girl ever forget such generosity and kindness of a favourite auntie?

I don't know how long she stayed in hospital. She came home still very weak. Papa set up her bed in the corner of their bedroom, so that they could tend to her during the night. Mama had placed the brass bell beside her sputum cup and I was the runner whenever Auntie Albe rang. My siblings and cousins popped in to see her from time to time, always in anticipation of leaving with candy. Wentzel visited her most evenings and weekends.

One evening she unexpectedly rose from her sickbed and joined the family for dinner. She had had little appetite for weeks. But this night she began to eat heartily and it appeared as though strength was miraculously flowing back into her body. After supper, Albe requested her favourite records be played on the battery-operated player. We were all ecstatic. Everyone babbled on about the miracle that was unfolding before our eyes,

In the morning, I was awakened by Mama's heart-wrenching wailing, "Albe! Albe! My child! My child!" During the course of the morning there was much commotion and confusion. I was sent across the field to summon Ray, Auntie Una and the rest of the family. Later someone told me that Auntie Albe had died. I did not quite know what to make of the news and had many questions milling around in my head. The days that followed were a blur, but I distinctly remember the day of the funeral. The little house was like a beehive.

A group of Albe's workmates from Poppies were busy down by the tap under the mulberry tree crafting leafy wreaths. As I wandered around at a loss among milling family and friends, I saw my mother come in through the kitchen door carrying a couple of freshly-made floral wreaths. Then she went limp and collapsed into a helpless heap, wreaths and all, on the floor. "*Oe Here,* Ray fainted! Mama, where's the smelling salts?" someone called to Mama clad in black, being comforted by visitors in the *voorkamer.*

"Who fainted?" she asked, her voice filled with concern.

"Ray," someone shouted across the din. Mama rushed to her bedroom for the smelling salts. Someone fixed her some sugar water. "Shame," another rejoined. "It's all been too much for her."

The piano, dining room table and sideboard had been removed from the living room to make space for the coffin. Women wearing black and men, dark suits with black mourning armbands, sat solemnly on chairs along the walls. The room smelt of sweet lilies, and a smell I could not identify then. Thinking back it was no doubt the embalming chemicals. The white coffin with silver handles rested on a wheeled stand, in the centre of the room. Wakes in the home were the norm in our community. Looking on through teary eyes a mourner whispered, "Doesn't she look peaceful?"

"Shame, she was so young. Tragic hey?" remarked another, "Poor Wentzel. Shame, he's so cut-up."

To me, Auntie Albe laid out in a lacy white nightgown, looked like Sleeping Beauty, and I was sure that if Uncle Wentzel bent down and kissed her on the lips she would awaken. It was explained to me that it was only her body in the coffin and that the real Albe had gone to heaven. Mourners packed out every room in the house, spilling out onto the shingled area outside. Pastor Valentine conducted the service. During the final hymn the undertakers screwed down the coffin lid. On it was a silver plaque inscribed Albertha Whitman 1938-1961.

After the final prayer, the mourners filed out of the front door, some piling into the string of cars parked along Acre Road, way past Mrs. Prodgers' shop, others crowding into two hired double-decker buses. The long procession to the graveyard befitted a dignitary. Strangers walking down the street stopped and men held their hats on their hearts, out of respect as was the custom then. After my Auntie's death, nothing in my halcyon world seemed quite the same. And for Mama, she would never witness a daughter having a 'white wedding.'

Chapter 16

The Group Areas

However tragic some events are, life does go on. While Auntie Albe's passing had left a void in my world, before too long, things were back to normal – well at least that's the way it seemed to me. But soon my world was to be shaken yet again. For the first time in my life, I would come face to face with the evil of apartheid.

One day, while Cousin Connie, Gracie Burns and I were playing housie-housie with our dolls at the end of the driveway, we noticed a mysterious-looking, bespectacled white man in an ill-fitting brown suit, slowly cycling by. Three pairs of curious eyes followed him as he turned into the Burns' driveway. He was a stranger to our neighborhood, a white stranger, certainly a new face to Connie and me at least. Under his fedora he wore a pencil-thin moustache on his upper lip. He cast us an unfriendly glance.

"Who's that?" Connie asked.

"It's the Group Area," Gracie replied matter-of-factly, like he was just a long lost unwelcome Uncle. 'Group Area' meant nothing to me but I sensed that he was no friend of ours. Later when Auntie Burns came over for tea she talked to Mama in unhappy tones. The grown-ups looked disheartened and worried. Whoever the 'Group Area' was, he must not have brought good tidings. Up till now our community had lived in relative harmony. If racism was present, we children didn't yet feel its effects.

Although the global media of the day rarely challenged South Africa's claim to being a democratic country, only White South Africans, constituting some twenty percent of the population, were permitted a vote. The somewhat onomatopoeic Afrikaans word, 'apartheid', simply means 'separateness'. The intent of apartheid was to keep the different race groups apart as far as practically possible. This meant enacting a raft of laws to achieve the grand design. Such major changes take time to both formulate and implement. So while the official birth of apartheid was 1948, its impact was more gradual and changes happened at different times in different places.

As I reflect back on that era, it seems unbelievable that supposed civilized people could even dream up such proposals let alone legislate them. 'Colour' was at the hub of the South Africa's political wheel. Everything revolved about this point. The overall racial division was 'white' and 'non-white'. The 'Non-Whites' were further sub-divided into 'Coloured,' 'Indian' and 'Black'. Naturally the Whites enjoyed the best of everything. The Coloureds and Indians came next with the Blacks, the indigenous tribal Africans on the bottom rung.

The Race Classification Act established a path whereby one could appeal to be racially reclassified. One must understand that the pigmentation of Coloureds ranged from as dark as ebony to as light as any 'blue-blooded European.' We "Coloureds" are a mixed race people coming from a melting pot of many diverse race groups. The criteria for determining where one belonged color-wise were diabolical to say the least.

Sometimes the Race Classification law backfired on even Afrikaners, as in the case of Sandra Laing from the eastern Transvaal town, Piet Retief. Some parents of children at a local all-white school complained that Sandra, whose biological parents were staunch Afrikaners, "looked Coloured." Much to the Laing's shame, Sandra was duly reclassified Coloured and promptly kicked out of her school. After much protest, she was "made white" again, but no white school would accept her. Ostracized by her community, she went to live among the Blacks in Soweto.

The Group Areas Act stipulated where the various race groups could or could not live. The choice areas were designated for Whites and the government erected concrete jungles on wind-swept, sandy plains on the city outskirts for the Coloureds and the Blacks.

The man on the bicycle had brought the Burns their eviction notice. Vasco had been declared a Whites only area. Mrs. Prodgers could stay, but the Burnses had seven days to get out.

"Tommy won't be able to carry on his taxi business, Mrs. Whitman," Minnie Burns lamented. "What are we going to do?" Her face was drawn and her pale blue eyes brimmed with tears. The City Council had assigned them a pokey house with a sandy, postage-stamp front yard in a cheek-by-jowl subdivision with narrow streets, cookie-cutter buildings and no amenities.

On a Friday morning, a week later, a Cape Town City Council truck backed into the Burns' driveway. Waiting in the wings was a menacing bulldozer. Bemused Non-White council workers unceremoniously heaved the Burns' possessions onto the truck. What could they do? They had hungry mouths to feed at home. The Burns family's mournful faces peered at Mama and me from behind the car windows. Auntie Burns was weeping. Mr. Burns slowly pulled away. I ambled along with Mama, clad in her ever-present apron, behind the bulky black Buick, Mama waving her handkerchief till they turned onto the Flinders Street intersection and were gone.

It all seemed rather unreal to me. Whatever explanations the grownups might have given us, as a nine year old, I could make little sense of it all. Segregation was not something I could comprehend, and the adults certainly didn't spell out the cold harsh realities – 'we are being moved from here because the government has decreed that this area is too good for Coloured people and is only good enough for whites'.

The bulldozer roared into action charging the Burns' house like an angry rhinoceros, tearing down the walls chunk by chunk - rushing, growling, devouring. A huge cloud of dust ascended from the rubble like a sacrificial offering to an angry god. In no time, the Burns' memories and all they had cherished were reduced to a pile of rubble.

One by one, families in our community suffered the same fate – the Alexanders, the Baptistes, the Macgregors, everyone in the row houses across the field, Mr. Ali's corner shop, Tanjeera – their existence in Vasco obliterated. The St. Albans church was razed and the bells of the musty, old City Mission silenced forever. Ray and Ted moved from the row houses to temporary make-shift accommodation erected on the Paulse family property in the uppity part of Vasco. They were yet to receive their eviction papers.

By the latter part of 1964, we were one of only a few families left in the immediate area. I was in my second year at Vasco Preparatory. The walk to school seemed so much further on my own. I never noticed the distance before, when there was still a bunch of us walking animatedly the mile to school The older kids used to tell scary stories about Chinamen in black cars kidnapping young children and taking them away to China forever. Now, on my solitary school walks, with little to distract me, I couldn't stop thinking about Chinamen. Sometimes, the nervous knots in my stomach started before I'd even left home. Mama would send me out the door neatly dressed in my navy tunic and white blouse, Panama hat on my head, brown school case in hand, cheerily waving goodbye. I'd get as far as Mr. Ali's boarded up shop then turn around and come charging back home banging on the door.

"What's the matter?" Mama would asked mystified

"The Chinamen are going to get me!" I'd cry.

"Don't be silly, there's no such thing, go to school now or you'll be late."

I'd go on my way as far as Mr. Ali's shop again, then turn around and scurry back home., "Go to school!" Mama would say again "I'm going to be late!" I'd wail.

"You are not late. But if you carry on like this, you *will* be. Now go!"

Although my school route took me past my paternal grandparents' house, I rarely stopped to visit them. No close relationship had formed between the Whitmans and Paulses and I, for all intents and purposes, was growing up as a Whitman. However, now that my parents were "camping" out on the Paulse property, albeit for a short period, I became a regular visitor. Strange that - my visiting my parents on my way home from school.

Towards the end of August, shortly before the entire Paulse clan had to pack up and move, I remember stopping by one afternoon seeing my mother propped up in bed, her face contorted in pain as an aunt helped her pump her engorged breasts. My youngest brother David lay bundled up beside her. I grew up a total innocent. I was vaguely aware of my mother's belly being 'fat' from time to time but I knew nothing about pregnancy. If you had told me she had a swallowed a watermelon I would've believed it. But I definitely wasn't that gullible to believe she had a baby in her belly! After all, I knew that nurses brought babies in their medicine bags.

It wasn't long after baby David's birth that Ray and Ted moved. I stood on the roadside watching the men loading their furniture onto a truck. Ray was shouting at the kids to keep out of the way. Soon they were all crammed into the truck, my father, mother and my five siblings. Before climbing aboard, Ray paused briefly, looked at me, and perfunctorily said, "Bye, you be a good girl for Mama, hey?"

And that was it. No hugs, no tears. Nothing.

I stood there motionless watching them pull away and drive off. I don't even know if I waved. But I do remember being overcome with immense sadness. If the rest of the Paulse relatives were about, I was oblivious of their presence. If Mama was with me, I don't remember, I just recall walking the mile back to Acre Road with a deep sense of loneliness and confusion.

It was not long after that, that One O Seven, Acre Road, was demolished. Peculiar as it may sound, I have no memory of the final days there. I'm sure we would have moved before the bulldozers came. I'm sure it would have been an emotional day. But for me it's a blank and perhaps that's just as well. Leaving the home you always knew is wrenching for most of us.

When it's a forced eviction where no crime's been committed, it adds to the pain. While I was too young to understand the injustice of our relocation, I did experience some of the emotional upheaval of it all. Had the Vasco community all been settled in the same area, I'm sure that would have softened the blow somewhat, but such emotional factors were no part of the government's relocation plans.

Chapter 17

The Cape Flats

The Cape Flats was the new address for most of Vasco's Coloureds, a concrete jungle of substandard housing on the outskirts of the city, built on sand with not a blade of grass in sight. No one wanted to be there but that was the only place the majority could afford from the meager compensation given them by the government. There was no sense of community. Crime was rife. The local newspaper reported senseless muggings, rapes and killings on an almost daily basis. People lived in fear of *skollie* gangs - idle, angry, vicious young thugs who roamed about looking for trouble. It was an age before crack, cocaine, speed and the myriad drugs in evidence today, but it was a time when *dagga* was smoked prolifically. The Africans and Coloureds had been smoking *dagga* (marijuana to the modern world) long before it became a problem in the western world. But its effects have not changed.

Uncle Jonathan's new house in the cramped subdivision of Bishop Lavis was dark, dingy and depressing, and smelled of damp concrete.

"I hate this place," said Auntie Ruth, Jonathan's wife, as she appeared through the kitchen door carrying a wooden tea tray Jonathan had crafted.

"And the sand!" she lamented. "Every time we open the door, the wind blows in the sand, I have to sweep every five minutes."

"Tsk-tsk-tsk," went Mama, shaking her head slowly from side to side.

"The damn *boere*," said Papa, "They make my blood boil!"

"Now Tom, don't upset yourself," Mama said gently.

"We all upset with the *boere*, Mummy," Uncle Jonathan chimed in. "But what can we do? We can't fight them. We must *maar* accept our lot."

"They're evil. Just plain evil," Mama replied. "But the Bible says we must love our enemies."

"Hmph," Papa sniffed, "How can you love evil?"

Changing the subject to defuse the tension, Mama asked Auntie Ruth,

"How's Minnie?" I had no idea then that Auntie Minnie Burns was Auntie Ruth's half sister. Holding the tray of tea and biscuits in front of her mother-in-law, Auntie Ruth replied *"Agh* Mummy, She's okay but Tommy is very depressed, he can't find work and now he's drinking."

"*Voeitog*," Mama sympathized, making small swirls in the tea she was holding with one hand as she stirred contemplatively with the other.

"And Vernon got the sack," Auntie Ruth continued. It wasn't his fault. The buses don't run on time and they always chock full. Sometimes he has to wait for over an hour. Then he has to take the train and always got to work late. So they sacked him."

"They make my blood boil, these damn *boere*!" Papa said crossly, biting hard into his biscuit.

We children stood around the tiny living room, our mouths covered with biscuit crumbs – eyeing the plate of goodies for more.

"Okay, you kids, you can't sit here in grownup company," Uncle Jonathan told us. "Go find a ball and play outside now and mind the cars!"

"To think of all the space they had to play in Vasco, hey? Now there's nowhere else for them to play," he said, looking plaintively at Mama. Playing in the street was new for me and I didn't like it.

We were more fortunate. Because of the size of our Vasco lot, we got a better settlement albeit that it was far less than the property was really worth. Papa was able to buy a piece of land in the already established Coloured suburb of Elsies River, a wrung up demographically from Bishop Lavis and Bonteheuwel. But when it came to crime it was no different from the rest of the Cape Flats.

The atmosphere was so different from our old neighbourhood. There was an almost tangible hostility in the air that even I, naïve as I was, could sense. And the people looked so different. In spite of everything, I felt immensely proud that we were now going to living in a brick and plaster house with hot and cold running water, no less. However, Papa, had the quirky notion that indoor toilets were unhygienic. It seemed God had not tempered his stubbornness. No amount of persuasion was going to change his mind about building an outside loo. The only saving grace was its being infinitely sturdier than its predecessor. To my recollection we were the only people in the street not connected to the city sewerage system. Knowing my grandfather it was probably because he did not want to pay the builder extra to have our sewer connected to the mains.

I suppose we had moved on but not much in my estimation. It was a source of embarrassment to me to have the CCC come pump out the sewerage tank every two weeks. Winter added another dimension to the toilet saga. The high clay content in the soil impeded drainage resulting in our yard being forever waterlogged, not a good situation with an outside toilet. But at least I didn't have to contend with reptiles anymore. If Papa thought he had saved money by not connecting a toilet to the mains, he thought he could save even more by keeping the hot water cylinder turned off during the week. We could bath on weekends only. We still had to boil water and carry it to the bathroom sink for our daily ablutions. I was twelve by now and if there was anything that really got under my skin, it was Papa and his crazy ideas about toilets and bathing. But I knew enough not to grumble or I would be told off in no uncertain terms.

Ever since moving to Elsies River, life was unsettled to say least. Uncle Robert's arrest, not long after our move was not only upsetting to me, but compounded the prevailing unhappiness of our being where we were. Uncle Robert, my mother's youngest brother had moved with us to Elsies River. He was very much a shadowy figure in my life. While he lived with Mama and Papa all through my growing years in Vasco, I saw little of him and really had no relationship with him. He was at least fifteen years older than I, was seldom at home and was typically doing his own thing.

It upset me to see Mama so distraught when we got word that Robert had been arrested on charges of *dagga* possession. He was sentenced to three months hard labor on a farm up country. He later told Mama and Papa that walking home that night, plain clothes white policemen stopped him and planted the weed when they patted him down. Whether his story was true or not, this was certainly very plausible given the reputation of South Africa's police. Papa found out the location in Villiersdorp and we planned a trip there for Mama to take Robert some clothes and food.

We drove on a Sunday afternoon through restful mountainous pastures and tidy patchwork vineyards – only this was no "joy" ride. My grandparents were anxious to see that their son was treated well. The Peugeot kicked up dust as its tires crunched up the gravel road leading to the farm. Mama had the farm's name written on the piece of paper in her hand. I was nervous about seeing the *baas* – I had visions of him – big, red and mean. I didn't see the *baas*. Papa spoke to the foreman who summoned Robert.

I'm not sure what I expected to see, but it was strange seeing my uncle in prisoner's khaki uniform, his long, boney face sun tanned.

"*Agh* Robert," Mama cried softly, holding on to him.

"*Moenie* worry *nie*, Mummy, they're treating me well," Robert said gently.

"And the *baas*, is he a good baas?" Papa asked.

"Ja," Robert replied, "So long as I do my work and I don't make trouble, I'm fine."

It wasn't long after that we made the trip to Villersdorp again, but this time to bring him home. His time had been shortened for good behavior.

Mama battled to establish a garden in the unfertile soil. Nothing would grow. It seemed when her prized velvety black lily she had transplanted from Vasco died, she died inwardly. She was never happy in Elsies River. She lost touch with most of her friends and sewing clients. She especially missed Mrs. Bowen, a close friend from the Vasco City Mission. I liked Mrs. Bowen, one of Mama's sewing clients. She was a kind, blue-eyed, powdery pink-cheeked white lady, who regularly dropped in for tea. But when she remarried, her husband forbade her to go to the Coloured area anymore.

Mama suffered from depression and her health began to deteriorate. She fussed about her "high blood" among various other ailments. In 1966, she had a mastectomy and was bedridden for about two weeks. This was her moment to garner all the sympathy she craved, for a couple of times she gathered the family around her sickbed to say farewell as she was convinced she was going to die. She lived for another couple of decades.

Chapter 18

Bad Happenings

Mrs. Adams' floors always gleamed. So clean were they, you could eat off them. I'd wager a bet that her house was probably the most immaculate on the block. I liked hanging out with her. She'd listen patiently to my teenaged ramblings while she ironed or prepared a meal. Dropping by to see her one day, Mr. Adams answered the door.

"Come in," he beckoned, flashing a friendly smile. I started walking to the kitchen to where I assumed his wife would be.

"Hello Mrs. Adams," I started to call, but got no reply.

"She's not here," Mr. Adams said quietly. He was right behind me. Placing his hands on my shoulders, he gently turned me toward him, started kissing me while steering me toward the back bedroom. I stood there passively as he kissed and fondled me.

Suddenly (and thankfully) there was the rattling of a key turning in a door.

"Quick!" he cried, in a state of panic. "Jump out the window!"

I simply did as I was told. I dropped down onto the sand below like a lump of lead. Stunned, I darted home and went straight to my room.

I heard the backdoor slam shut and footsteps coming down the passage. I knew it was Ted. I was sitting on my bed, my shoulders hunched. He spoke softly, telling me another neighbour had told him he saw me jumping out of the Adams's window. If ever I wanted the earth to swallow me, it was then. He sat down beside me, and listened calmly to the story I told. I was flabbergasted by what happened next. "Let me see where he touched you." I awkwardly point to my breasts. "Let me see." He stared for what seemed like an eternity, got up and left the room.

From that moment on, I loathed him. In my head I screamed, "I hate you," but outwardly, I just sat there like a dumb animal ready for the slaughter. Why didn't I protest? Why didn't I scream? Why didn't I fight back? And why didn't my father go knock Mr. Adams's block off? I was numb from the violation and seething from my father's betrayal. Sadly this wasn't the only occasion when my father made such an overture. While there wasn't anything significant of a physical nature, and the two incidences were short-lived, the internal impact it had remains with me to this day. I was also a little older on the second occasion and had by then gained the confidence to protest. And when I did, he stopped. For the rest of his life, he pretended that nothing had ever happened. Some years later when I told my mother of these things, her matter-of-fact response was, "Your father is only human."

Was I jinxed or something? I began to wonder, because even from a very young age, bad happenings seemed to have a pattern of following me. Growing up I was just never in a safe place physically or emotionally. My community had very prudish attitudes about sex. The subject was never directly talked about. As I child I came to understand sex as being something bad. When we saw animals copulating, we were told not to look. The dogs were doing 'rude.' Sex was known as "doing rude." Men and women did 'rude.' What exactly the "rude" thing entailed, was a complete mystery to me.

Simms was a family friend (I think he was connected with the church.) A seemingly affable young adult, my grandparents treated him like a son, but there was something about him that didn't sit right, even for me as a five-year-old. The one thing I can remember of him from Vasco days was the time he bought me sweets from Mr. Ali's shop and on the way to the store his talking about his pee-pee. Beyond that my mind draws a blank.

Five years later, Simms resurfaced in my life, now a boarder at my grandparents in Elsies River. We were on friendly terms, but given of our age difference, we had very little interaction but I do recall that his furtive glances and beguiling smiles at the dinner table made me feel somewhat uneasy. In today's parlance one might say his behaviour was creepy.

One afternoon when Mama was out, I found myself alone with Simms in his bedroom. Our conversation somehow turned to that "doing rude" thing. Even by aged ten, I was still incredibly naïve about such matters. I didn't feel at all afraid when Simms drew the curtains and had me lay on his bed. In my mind this was kind of a game like playing "housie-housie." He was calm and very matter-of-fact, like someone doing an experiment. Fortunately, he didn't follow through with intercourse. He told me to wait till I was a bit older, whatever that meant.

This incident didn't sit right with me. A couple of days later, when my grandmother was sitting by the kitchen table sewing, I told her about what had transpired with Simms. Her face went ashen as she stopped dead in her tracks. She quizzed me for more details. I didn't realise the gravity of the matter till my grandfather got home from work. When Simms came through the door, he was summoned to my grandparents' bedroom.

Sitting in the kitchen I could hear them interrogating him. He was lucky not to have encountered the Papa of old because there were no raised voices. Simms told them I had been tempting him. My grandparents duly tossed Simms out by the ear there and then. I was told to get my cardigan

and then we went off in Papa's old Peugeot to the doctor
in Goodwood. I lay on the examination table not knowing
what all the fuss was about and why the old bespectacled
White doctor had to examine my private parts. It was all
highly embarrassing for me. With the doctor done, I was
taken back to the waiting room. My grandparents were
clearly relieved that everything was all right and I had come
to no harm. I was fortunate on two accounts; that I hadn't
been physically violated and that my grandparents believed
me.

That same evening we went to Auntie Una's in Kensington
where Ray and Ted were renting one of the bedrooms.
Mama told the adults what had happened. When she told
Ray that according to Simms I had tempted him, I heard
her tell Mama, "Mummy must beat her." My older cousins
having heard about this sordid piece of gossip, surrounded
me like I had had an encountered with an alien from Mars,
and grilled me for the gory details. I felt dreadfully awkward
and shamed beyond words.

As an adult, in talking to other females with whom I grew
up, I learned this was simply a part of the way things were
then in our culture. I heard story after story of women who
were sexually abused as girls. One friend whose mother was
deceased and father had abandoned her, recounted how she
was raped as a child, by her guardian. When she complained
to his wife, the woman gave her a mischievous laugh, saying,
"Ooh, he's made a woman out of you."

At a guess, most young people in North America would
deem their sixteenth birthdays as one of the highlights in their
lives. I wonder how many can report that on their sixteenth
birthday they were assailed by robbers. That's exactly what
happened to me on my sixteenth birthday. Toting a shopping
bag with new duds I had purchased from Edgar's department
store, I was walking home down Tenth Avenue.

I was in good spirits about my little shopping spree to which I treated myself with the money I had earned working at a hat factory during the winter school holidays. I felt like I had walked right off the fashion pages of *Fair Lady* magazine sporting a fashionable outfit and felt especially groovy peering out oversized blue-tinted, gold-rimmed sunglasses. Half way along, I noticed a gang of youths in the distance sauntering toward me. I crossed the street to avoid them and to my horror, they did the same.

They had me in their cross hairs; I couldn't think what course of action I needed to take. They obviously had it in for me, whatever I did. So I just kept walking hoping for the best. I recognised the ringleader as the "bad girl" who had gone to my primary school. I held my breath instinctively like one being swarmed by a dark cloud of malicious hornets. As I ran their gauntlet, I felt my lovely sunglasses being snatched off my face. In that split second my mind roiled as I waited for them to grab my shopping bag. I braced myself to feel the sharp end of a knife stick into my flesh. Instead the bad girl told me menacingly that next time I wouldn't be so lucky.

The wind had whooshed out of me like a burst tire. I continued on home feeling grievously violated and deflated. If I had birthday celebrations or presents to which to look forward, it might have softened the blow somewhat. (My parents were quite unsentimental about such things.) This was by far the worst birthday I can remember. On the other hand, it might have been the best because in retrospect the greatest gift I was given on my "Sweet Sixteenth" birthday was the gift of my guardian angel prevailing in that battle. The outcome could easily have been tragic. It took over half my life overcoming the notion that bad things happened to me because I was bad and undeserving.

Chapter 19

Changes

I was nine years old when I started standard one at Elnor Primary School, in Elsies River. Unlike Vasco, the walk to school was a mind field. No sidewalks, just narrow pot-holed shoulders with traffic whizzing by. And when a Golden Arrow double decker came hurtling by I was terrified the draft would suck me right under its wheels. It was not uncommon to see a group of people gathered round some figure sprawled on the asphalt.

School uniforms were the norm in South Africa right across the colour spectrum. At Elnor it was green tunics with white shirts and school neckties for the girls, and gray flannel shorts, white shirts, neckties and green v-neck sweaters for the boys. Going to school that first day was scary. I knew no one. I'm sure I looked very lost as I tried to blend into the sea of regimented green. I soon found out that things here would be very different from Vasco Prep - no carefree days playing with my classmates under large shady trees. In fact there wasn't a tree in sight just a large scrubby field. And to my great disappointment, no twice-a-week strawberry-flavored milk like my old Vasco school. Elnor Primary School was a low prefabricated utilitarian building in stark contrast to the beautiful colonial style of my previous school. It was cold and regimented, and to add to my discomfort, we were now taught in Afrikaans only.

Singing the Afrikaans national anthem, *Die Stem* van Suid Afrika, was something new for me. I've always loved singing so it is little wonder that I heartily belted out the anthem. I was too young to appreciate how farcical this was – singing the praises of the Afrikaner and the nation where I was at best a second class citizen. And for good measure, we were required to learn *Die Stem* by heart! I survived my first year and performed fairly well scholastically, placing first in my class and receiving an award at the annual prize-giving. It was a hard-cover picture book about a garden gnome, *Bam Die Dwergie*. What a cheesy title. I remember it, not because of its content, but because it was an award I received in front of the whole assembly; a real feel-good occasion for a newbie, and being affirmed in any way was something I craved.

Fortunately, it didn't take long for me to make friends. When Brenda Geyer and Merle Mitchell offered to trade sandwiches at lunchtime, I knew I was in. We walked the same route to school. We were never bosom buddies but Brenda, I remember because she often had *Marie* biscuits and cheese in her lunchbox. She was a light eater and so on occasions I would be the recipient of her yummy left-overs. And did I ever love *Marie* biscuits and cheese. As for Merle, I committed my first sin of covetousness over her lovely, long, sleek, brown hair.

Regardless of race or nationality, hair has always been an issue in terms of style, condition and appearance, with women. But among women of colour in South Africa, it was an obsession, something seared into our psyche. At school the girls with the long sleek hair were picked as marching majorettes, representing their schools at the inter-school mini-Olympic track meets. If you had a *kroeskop* you didn't have a prayer. Forget about entering any beauty pageant – forget about entering anything if you had nappy hair.

So the name of the game was do whatever it takes to straighten your hair - ironing, swirling and when all else failed the *WellaStrate* treatment. These weren't simple fixes. They were all-day productions. Girls would turn down dates to work on their hair. Ironing was the quickest method but it wasn't for everyone. On top of that, it was weather dependent. Only girls with long hair could iron and if the weather was damp and foggy, then forget it. Ironing required laying brown paper over your long hair and smoothing it with a clothes iron.

Swirling was the most popular method and wasn't as weather dependent as ironing. You washed your hair, rolled it in curlers, let it dry and brushed it out. Using the leg of discarded pantyhose, you pulled it over your head, bank robber style, turning it in a swirling motion around the head. Then you let it be. The longer you kept the stocking on, the smoother the result. It wasn't a pretty sight, but it did the job.

By the early seventies the *Wella* hair brand came out with *WellaStrate* for girl with very *kroes koppe*. It stank of rotten eggs when applied a smelly business, but it made those girls happy. Even when the Afro style was trendy, straightened hair was still preferable.

The hair fetish was not just the Coloured girls' domain. Apartheid also got into the hair business. Straight hair could equal White. *Kroes* hair definitely equaled Non-white. Under the Race Classification Act, the government made provision for people to appeal their classification. For starters you had to be a very light-skinned Coloured to stand a chance. One of the criteria was the "pencil test." This involved inserting a pencil in your hair to see whether it was kinky or nappy enough to hold the pencil when you bent forward. If it fell out, lucky you, you could be on your way to being White. If it stuck, unlucky you. You were back to where you started. This might sound totally ludicrous, but believe me, under apartheid extraordinary things happened.

The sad reality was that situations existed where members of the same family who had different hair textures found themselves in different race groups as a result of this test. Besides causing obvious emotional trauma within those families, it also presented serious consequences for families as regards South Africa's Population Registration Act, Pass Law, Group Areas Act. It tore families apart.

But I digress. Although I'm sure I did do some fun things at Elnor Primary School, I'm hard pressed to recall any. But sensitive as I was, it's the hurtful things that always come to mind. The time a school peer smacked me in the face for supposedly telling tales about her. I was on my way back from the Bubbie shop carrying a gallon can of paraffin. Going to the store for paraffin was the bane of my life. Papa was obsessed with limiting the use of electricity to save money and so the Primus stove was still used. Other kids bought sweets and Beatles and Elvis memorabilia I bought stupid paraffin!

As bold as brass she marched up to me. I didn't even see her hand come up to my face, but I felt the sharp sting on my cheek. "That's for *skinnering* about me," she hissed.

And with that she turned on her heels and marched away. Stunned, I quickened my pace home, choking back the tears till I reached the back door.

"What's the matter?" Mama inquired when I started bawling.

"A girl from school smacked me in the face!" I blurted incoherently. I cried not only about the assault, but also about the blasted paraffin oil that had spilled onto my hand and leg during the attack. I hated the paraffin, and I hated Elsies River.

What made it worse was I never said anything bad about her. It was actually all about a school yard disagreement as to who was the greatest, Elvis Presley or Cliff Richard! If memory serves me right I picked Cliff Richard. Man, I always backed the wrong pony. Uncle Robert said I should have smacked her back. But I just never had it in me to fight back.

I was now at the age where subconscious emotions were starting to rise to the surface. It bothered me that my classmates had their parents' surname and I had a different name to Mama who was in every respect, except biologically, my mother. I wanted my world to be more ordered. If I was going to live with my grandparents, I wanted to be a Whitman. I didn't want to be singled out, "Why are you Jennifer Paulse and not Jennifer Whitman." I didn't verbalize these feelings to anyone but I wrestled with them internally. Hmm, maybe one day I'd be Jennifer Collison.

Chapter 20

The Collisons

My struggle with identity wouldn't go away. I needed a world that made sense to me - a world with a perfect family to which I could belong. And in my South Africa, a perfect family naturally had to be White. Enter, the Collisons, a name that I had plucked from the air simply because it had a nice ring to it. Mrs. Collison, the matriarch had no first name. She had smiling blue eyes and wore her hair swept back elegantly, like princess Grace of Monaco. She was kindness personified. Mr. Collison was a more introverted, rather non-descript avuncular gentleman who busied himself in the background doing stuff business tycoons do.

They had four children. The oldest son, Basil, wore horn-rimmed glasses and a doctor's coat. Next came Iris, a nurse, who dutifully stood by her older brother healing the infirm. Veronica, the vivacious actress, sported flicked-up auburn hair and was always very fashionably dressed. And then there was Neville, the love of my life. He had a Beatle haircut like John Lennon, but his hair was blonde. He had a playful sense of humour and loved to tease me and I loved it when he did. But in my vivid twelve-year-old imagination these characters were very real. How on earth did I come up with a cringe-worthy name like Neville. But there he was, the love of my life.

I even told a playmate that the Collisons were visiting and that they had come from England. Did she want to meet them? I let her come as far as the closed bedroom door, letting her wait in the hallway as I slowly opened it just enough for me to poke my head in. 'Mrs. Collison, my friend would like to meet you', I whispered through the crack. 'You're resting? Okay, we'll come back tomorrow,' I said, closing the door softly.

"She's resting," I whispered to my friend waiting in anticipation. Where was Dr. Phil when I needed him?

I went so far as to "introduce" the Collisons to my siblings. I had gone with Mama and Papa to visit my parents now living in the Kensington housing estate. While the grownups were enjoying cups of tea indoors, my siblings and I sat on the *stoep* in the sun, our mouths working over Stars pink taffy I bought from the Bubbie's shop.

"I'm going to be adopted," I proclaimed out of the blue, my teeth and tongue deliciously neon pink.

"What's adopted?" asked Alan now clearly interested.

"I'm going to live with Mrs. Collison. They're very rich. You should see their house. It's a mansion. It's got twenty bedrooms and ten toilets!"

"Yes-like-it. Ten toilets!" Alan could hardly believe his ears - his amber brown eyes were as big as saucers. "A mansion?"

"Yes," I continued. "And you should see their driveway; it's as long as the whole of Ninth Avenue. And their land is as big as the whole of Kensington. And their dining room table is as long as this house".

Alan stared at me in amazement. His brow wrinkled into furrows then suddenly relaxed. His face took on the self-satisfied look of one about to set a trap in motion.

"How do you know?"

"Because I saw it with my own eyes, stupid!"

"Do you know how to get to their house? Can Dada take us there in the car?"

"No man, it's too far. It's in England."

"England!" "You been to England!" His brow began to wrinkle again, eyes wide with wonder. "You lie. You can't go to England in a car."

"Who said I went in a car to England?" I replied smugly, "I went in Mr. Collison's aeroplane, man. I told you they were super rich. They are so rich they have their own super fast jet plane."

Four mesmerized brown faces hung onto my every word.

"The Collisons are so nice. There's Mrs. Collison; she's so nice. When I see her, I always run to her and she gives me a big hug and a big kiss. Mr. Collison likes me too. They have four children; Basil and Iris and Veronica and Neville. Basil, is a doctor, and Iris, is a nurse and Veronica, she's an actress and Neville, he goes to the university. Neville is so handsome and we're going to get married. He looks like Mark Condor from the *boekies*."

"But Mark Condor is white," Alan interjected.

"The Collisons are white," I said nonchalantly.

"Yes-like-it! And they going to, what you say, adopt you?"

"Yes." My eyes sparkling with glee.

"Will you be white?"

"Yes."

My siblings' eyes were riveted on me as though they had just experienced an epiphany of sorts. This was all too good to be true for Alan. All at once he was transported back to earth. Skepticism beset him.

"You lie," he blurted out. "You telling lies."

"I'm not lying," I replied smarmily.

"I'm going to ask Mama," said my brother, throwing down the gauntlet.

"Go. Go ask Mama," I dared him.

Alan took up the challenge and called my bluff.

Jumping up, he ran into the kitchen, where the adults were talking, Sharon and Desmond in tow. I chose to lurk in the doorway at a safe distance.

Mama paused in mid-sentence, when Alan gingerly tapped her arm.

"Alan, I am talking. It's rude to interrupt when someone is talking," she said primly.

"Hey!" Ray bellowed sharply, "Go play outside!"

Alan would normally have obeyed instantly for fear of getting a clout on the head. But this matter was much too serious. He desperately needed to know the answer to his burning question.

"Mama, Jenny says she went on a plane to England and Mrs. Collison is going to adopt her and she's going to marry Neville," Alan blurted.

"Alan!" Ray barked more ferociously this time, "Go play outside and stop talking rubbish!"

Alan knew best not to pursue the matter any further and we all retreated to the *stoep*.

"You lied, man!" Alan exclaimed, "Yes, Mummy says you talking rubbish," Sharon chimed in.

"Mama doesn't know about it. Mrs. Collison must still come talk to her about it," I insisted and abruptly changed the subject. "Let's play hide and seek."

Whenever I drifted into my "Neverland" the Collisons were there to indulge me. Neville always playfully teased me. The Collisons were the Von Trapps and Mary Poppins rolled into one. Although I was twelve, I was the girl in the gazebo in *The Sound of Music*, "sixteen going on seventeen." Neville had "told" me that he was going to wait for me to grow up and take me to England and marry me. The Collisons were the fix I needed to make right in my life all that was wrong.

Chapter 21

I Wanna Go Home

"Go home!" Ray had yelled at me, once, when we all still lived in Vasco. I'd come over to play with my siblings while Ray and Ted were taking their customary Sunday afternoon nap. On the Formica-topped kitchen dresser sat a colourful tin of Baumann's cookies. It was a special Christmas bonus tin with vivid, crisp images of the delectable assortment of its contents. The temptation proved too much, and I clambered onto a chair and then the dresser reaching for the container. Either it proved too heavy or I simply lacked the finesse of a cat burglar, but to my horror the tin of cookies came tumbling down clipping my head and crashing to the floor.

The commotion aroused my slumbering parents, and Ray came thundering through the door. She grabbed a piece of loose-lying plank nearby and swung it at my behind. "*Jou verdomde kind!* Don't you come here and be naughty like this. Go home!" Frightened and bewildered, I rushed out the door as fast as my feet could carry me, and ran across the field back to my grandparents' house. I never really knew where "home" truly was.

This feeling came to the fore years later in Elsies River. It was a Saturday afternoon as I lay on my stomach on my bed listening to the Hit Parade on the radio, when a doleful, twangy, country tune really got to me. Whenever it played it stirred up a yearning and sadness deep within that nagged at me. It was called *I Wanna Go Home*. Mama was clattering away on her old sewing machine on the kitchen table. My heart was throbbing rapidly in my chest as I summoned up the courage to broach this subject. "Mama?"

"Huh-mmm?" she replied absent-mindedly, without looking up.

"I wanna go home."

Mama's hand froze on the handle, her puzzled bespectacled eyes looked up from the unfinished garment to me standing in front of the kitchen sink, twirling my braids,

"What do you mean, you want to go home?"

"I want to go live with my Mummy and Daddy."

I'm sure this must have come like a bolt out of the blue for Mama who had raised me for twelve years. She got up and put the kettle on for tea, not saying anything for a while. "I'll have to talk it over with your parents then," Mama said eventually. Suppertime was rather subdued. Mama was pensive and I felt uneasy keeping my gaze on my food as I ate. I was somewhere within earshot when I heard her breaking the news to Papa. "Well, we'll have to talk to Ray and Ted, then," I heard him say. A trip was made in Papa's old Peugeot, and arrangements were subsequently made for me to move "home" with my parents.

By now Ted and Ray had their own house on the Kensington housing estate that they bought on the Council's thirty-year-mortgage payment plan. Of the few modest designs offered by the Council, Ted and Ray plummed for the most basic model. But it didn't stay that way for too long. Bit by bit, additions were added.

These started out as DIY projects but invariably ended up with a professional having to come in and complete or redo the job. Ted's do-it-yourself drive was motivated more by thoughts of the money he could save rather than any illusions of being Mister Fix-it. His weakness was lack of planning. He would invariably jump feet first into a project and then it was a matter of sink or swim. One or more of my brothers would be seconded as work site gophers, primarily as cement mixers.

His most ambitious undertaking was extending the boys' bedroom and adding a 'granny flat' or as we called it in South Africa, 'servant's quarters. ' Once work started sighs of exasperation and back and forth shouting began.

"Mix man! Mix!" Ted would shout when the boys slackened off.

"But my arms are tired, Dada," came the rejoinder.

"Hey! I'll give you tired, now mix!" Ted's round, shiny face morphing into a dark scowl as he paused from his trowel work on the brick wall in front of him.

On and on it went until finally the walls were up. Now plastering requires a lot of skill and know- how, but you couldn't tell that to Ted. He flicked dollops of plaster onto the wall, as he'd seen masons do and then began smoothing it with his trowel. But no sooner done, the mixture slithered down forming messy globs on the floor. After several such attempts, he tossed the trowel down in frustration, bent down and picked up handfuls of cement, smearing it back on the wall. My brothers stood by laughing at this spectacle.

"Hey!" Ted cried out, exasperated. "You didn't mix the *verdomde* plaster as I told you! It's too thin!"

"We mixed it good, Dada, it's not our fault!"

Needless to say, Ted eventually enlisted a skilled plasterer to complete the job. The four boys now had a bit more room to spread out and the "servant's quarters", crude as it was, was rented out for extra income.

Just when I thought he'd learned his lesson about his DIY limitations, his old bugbear – lack of planning - again bit him in the rear. He engaged Brother Daniels from the church to paint the kitchen and bathroom. Brother Daniels worked on cargo ships that took him to exotic ports around the world. My parents had a kitsch souvenir gondola he had brought back from Venice that took pride of place in the glass display cabinet attached to the hi-fi radiogram/record player. When Brother Daniels was back on land on long leave, he would don his odd-job hat. Come Friday, with his job well done and his painting kit all packed up, Brother Daniels was ready to be paid. Ted emerged from his bedroom looking rather ill-at-ease holding up two of his suits draped over clothes hangers. Embarrassment was written all over his face.

"Brother," he began awkwardly, "I don't have the money to pay you this week, man, but I can give you these suits as part payment and I'll give you the money next week."

Clearly miffed, the mild-mannered church brother staring through his thick Coke-bottle-based glasses, replied, "No man, Brother Ted you promised to pay me when the job was done. How am I supposed to feed my family on suits?"

"I'm sorry, man, brother, but I just don't have the money this week."

I don't know how the matter was resolved, but after that I never saw Brother Daniels ever again. And Ted could forget about getting the latest gospel records Brother Daniels used bring back from America. Things certainly operated differently at the house of Paulse.

Chapter 22

Life At One Sixty Six

From my twelve-year-old perspective I felt that going home would fulfill the emotional void of 'a place to belong' that was so acutely lacking. Of course, I had no capacity for appreciating what this step would actually entail, or the dynamics of going from being an only child in my grandparents' house to being thrust in among five siblings. I was soon to find out that the Paulse's household was in stark contrast to Mama's.

There were no set rules, and boundaries changed constantly. One day you could get away with a trespass and the next you'd get a whipping for it. Shouting, arguing, ridiculing, teasing and put-downs, were the norm. Mealtimes were chaotic and void of table manners. Everyone had to fend for himself. Conversations around the Formica-topped table were conducted through muffled mouthfuls of food and when it came to food, Ted never liked to be kept waiting. He would habitually tap his index finger on the table grumbling impatiently, "*Kom nou, waarsie kos.*"

On week days with eight in the house and one cramped bathroom I quickly learned the benefit of being first in line. Ablutions done and back in my room I shared with Sharon, I'd always part the curtains to do a weather check. Table Mountain in the distance was my barometer. If clear and cloudless, it was going to be a nice day. If shrouded in heavy clouds, I knew it best to take my umbrella.

The standard pattern was that we kids had to fend for ourselves in the mornings.

I'd fix myself tea and toast that I'd slather with *Koo* apricot jam. I preferred *Melon 'n Ginger* jam but it never lasted long in our house. School lunch would be two slices of buttered bread and whatever spread was available in the fridge. It was a special treat if there was leftover *Bobotie*, (leftovers being a rarity) – another reason to get up first. The rest of my siblings would wander in one by one, following the same mode – tea and toast and fixing their school lunches.

On the occasions when Ray did get up, she'd cook a pot of *mielie pap* or oatmeal porridge, neither of which I much cared for. Toothless, she'd schlep into the kitchen wearing a swirl stocking on her head, her false teeth still soaking in a glass of water in the bedroom. She had a double persona – the pious church-lady look and the *skelbek* Coloured *vrou* – and this was not the former. The irony was that mornings ran much smoother when we were left to our own devices. With Ray up and about there'd be cries of "Mummy, where's my school shirt?" "Mummy, I don't have a shirt either!"

"It's in the clothes hamper," Ray would reply through flapping lips.

"But there are dirty clothes in there."

"No, they're clean. Bring them here so I can iron them," she'd say blearily.

Unlike Mama, Ray had no set system for doing laundry or housework. So the boys would habitually be ferreting for something to wear at the last minute. The schools had strict codes when it came to uniforms. If you didn't comply, you'd be let off with a warning or at worst be sent home to dress appropriately. Alan was always the last to get up. He loved his sleep. You could bank on hearing Ray's shrill voice shouting down the passage. "Alaaan! *Staan op!* " I never saw Ted in the mornings. He was now working for Lewis Furniture where his hours were flexible and he had the luxury of sleeping in.

With Mama I enjoyed undivided attention and affection, not so with Ray. She lacked empathy, was undemonstrative and was really quite unsentimental about children. In reflection, I'm sure my expectations were much too high and I had no way of knowing what it entailed struggling to raise five kids. I think I could have put up with her sharpness, but it was her lack of affection and affirmation that were wounding. But for all that, it never crossed my mind to move back to Mama's. Somehow the struggle I was having fitting in at One Sixty Six outweighed the loneliness I had begun to feel at Mama's coupled with my yearning for a relationship with my biological family. But at least Mama's door was always open when I needed solace.

Before my arrival at One Sixty Six, Alan had been the pack leader. Inevitably sibling rivalry arose between the two of us. He resented taking orders from me, the 'interloper.' I knew I had overstepped the bounds the time I called him "*kaffir,*" his complexion being significantly darker than mine. In retaliation he raised his leg swiftly kicking me judo-style in the stomach. I doubled over in pain gasping for breath. Mama was the only one who could make it right. Tears coursed down my cheeks as I walked the fifteen minutes it took to get to Auntie Una's house. I told her what Alan had done and I wanted to go to Mama's but had no bus fare.

"But Alan mustn't kick you, man," Auntie Una said sympathetically. She gave me some coins and I walked the mile up Twelfth Avenue to the bus stop on Voortrekker Rd.

There was nothing in Kensington that remotely resembled its London namesake. It was a leafless, cheerless suburb extremely exposed to Cape Town's infamous southeaster, as evidenced by detritus plastered on wire-linked fences. Rowdy children shouted and laughed raucously, and *skollies* loitered on street corners wolf-whistling at pretty girls and sometimes worse. "Interfering" it was called. It wasn't a safe place for females to be alone. Rape and assaults ran rampant in our communities. And then there was the challenge of negotiating Elsies River's Halt Road with no sidewalks and treacherous drivers. Looking back, I'm amazed how I ever got anywhere in one piece.

Mama was surprised to see me. She listened to my tale of woe and it was a given that I would stay for supper. Mama's food was always comforting. Afterwards she and Papa drove me back to Kensington. Papa reprimanded Ted, "You must teach your boys that it's just not on to kick girls in the stomach."

When Mama and Papa left, I was very unpopular.

"Next time you don't go running to Mama and Papa to complain, you hear?" Ted scolded me. Ray stood beside him glaring fiercely as I slinked to the bedroom. What I wanted to say in my defense was that it was no use complaining to them, as they would only dismiss it as trivial. But as usual I kept quiet.

Puberty can be tumultuous at best, and it doesn't take much to be embarrassed. In one's self-consciousness and awkwardness the best one can hope for is a soft place to land. With Ray there was no such place. Her seemingly innocuous comments could sting like barbs. The time I tripped over my tongue trying to join in the adult conversation and Ray's, "Jennifer talks so indistinct," irritable response was soul-destroying. At moments like those I wished I could have just vaporized. But to be fair, there were the odd throw-away comments that I grabbed onto with both hands. "I like the way you write the letter 'f'," she said matter-of-factly. That this insignificant statement is seared in my memory to this day bears evidence of the affirmation I so craved.

Ray and Ted's blistering rows, usually about money, subsided for a while when she went to work at Punky's, the new supermarket on Voortrekker Road. Ray employed a live-in maid/child minder (who shared the bedroom with Sharon and me). Rosie was a nineteen-year-old country girl who became corrupted by the big city. At bedtime, whether she thought Sharon was too young to understand, or whether she thought Sharon was asleep, Rosie would regale me with tales of her sexual escapades. They were certainly intriguing, although I was still too green to know what it all meant.

Before long Rosie had gotten herself pregnant and after four months when she could no longer conceal her swelling belly, Ray gave her the sack. She had two weeks to work out her notice and find somewhere else to stay. She managed to cut that time short when one morning, in a very ticked-off mood, Rosie had yanked Desmond from his warm bed, scolding him for wetting it. She dragged him into the bathroom, plonking him into a bath of cold water to teach him a lesson. Desmond's gasps and cries brought Ray rushing to the bathroom.

"He wet the bed again, Mrs. Paulse," Rosie offered.

A high pitched, "Are you mad?" was immediately followed by a "whack" sound.

"What's the matter with you, huh? How dare you ill-treat my children, hey?"

Stunned, Rosie stood in the passage way holding the side of her face, her narrow eyes brimming with tears.

"You take your stuff, right now, and you get out of my house!" Ray screamed, her arm ramrod straight, pointing to the door.

"But I have nowhere to go, Mrs. Paulse," Rosie wailed.

"That's not my damn problem." Ray's stare was like menacing daggers.

"Out of my house! Out!"

Rosie sought shelter at a sympathetic neighbor and a few months later gave birth to a baby boy. She didn't stay in town for long and was never heard of again. The one good thing about Rosie's stay with us was that for a brief period the house was always reasonably tidy.

With Rosie turning out to be no Mary Poppins, my parents thought that I was now old enough to step in as child-minder. I was a conscientious kid and took my responsibility very seriously. And besides which, this presented a great opportunity for me to win favor with my mother.

I even went so far as to wash and wax the kitchen floor. We didn't have an electric buffer, so I got innovative. I found a disused threadbare blanket and had the small boys sit on it while I slid them around till the floor shone like new. They squealed with laughter as I pulled and whipped them about. It was Desmond's turn to be the buffer. Spinning him around with a little too much vigour, his body slammed into the kitchen dresser. Thankfully he was not hurt but a glass bowl on the shelf wasn't so fortunate. All I could think of was the smack I was going to get when Ray got home.

"Ooh," she said gleefully as she came through the door still in her yellow Punky's uniform, "The floor looks nice."

My hard work not only got me kudos but also outweighed the loss of the broken bowl.

When I got home from school it was my job to straighten up the kitchen. The cramped counter often crawled with ants gorging themselves on splatters of jam and trails of breadcrumbs left over from the breakfast scrum. And there'd be food-encrusted dishes crowding the sink and frequently a pot or two on the stove from the morning oatmeal or the previous night's stew.

But the dishes could wait. What was so much more important was tuning in to the serialized Afrikaans radio soaps. These melodramas came on between two and four o'clock during weekdays. It would always be a mad dash from school to make sure I didn't miss an episode. There was no television then. So I at least had the luxury of painting my own picture of the various characters. Alan was also really into the soaps. We would sit on the carpet, backs against the sofa, riveted to every word coming out of the Hi-Fi Radiogram. Whether or not Alan visualized the characters, I never knew, but I could certainly see it all – Kobus, of *Die Bannelinge*, rugged, muscular, suntanned and handsome on his horse,

riding beside Miedtz the stubborn, red-headed beauty. In
the story line, there was an obvious chemistry between the
two. But soap writers being notorious for drawing things out,
it took forever for the kiss to come. The suspense was killing.
As soon as the show ended at four o'clock I'd spring into
action frantically cleaning up, and then braising onions and
meat in preparation for the *bredie* Ray would complete when
she got home.

Friday, pay day, gave us a break from boring stews. We
could look forward to a fish supper. Of all the places I've lived
in the world, nothing compares to fish trawled off the Cape
coastline – stockfish, maasbankers, kingklip, kabeljo, and the
big daddy of them all – snoek. Those were the days when
fish hawkers along the main road dangled three- foot snoek
to entice passing traffic. You could buy a snoek for sixpence
and, boy, was it delicious fried up, long tube of roe and all.

Whenever Ted had the opportunity he'd go with a group
of friends at the crack of dawn to Kalk Bay to do rock angling.
Ancient mariners didn't name Cape Town's rough seas the
'Cape of Storms' for nothing, because every so often one
would hear of an angler swept off the rocks by a powerful
breaker. Thankfully, Ted and his mates always got home
in one piece bearing wonderful *fruit de mare*. Ray used to
say, "*Oe die vis panne skree, van aand,*" (The fish pans are
screaming tonight.)

Our family simply loved fish. That I started cooking at
a fairly young age is what sparked my love of the culinary
arts. Although, my first attempt at frying fish was a disaster.
Running late in picking Ray up from the supermarket, one
evening, Ted left me in charge of cooking the fish for supper.
Now you can't tell a thirteen year old to cook fish without
leaving explicit instructions. You can't employ a one-method-
fits-all to cooking fish. So still having Kobus and Miedtz
of *Die Bannelinge* on the brain, I plonked the stock fish in
unheated oil in the frying pan. Bad start. The end product

was a fish hash offering. To this day, whenever I'm frying fish, I can still hear Ted's scolding, "Look what you've done to the fish! What, do you have snot for brains?"

That jab never put me off any seafood, though. I could happily subsist on the stuff.

Many parents in those days in my community, lacking good parental skills trying to raising large families, let alone struggling to make ends meet, often took out their frustrations on their children. Perhaps because of my sensitive nature I took my father's brusqueness and irritability too much to heart. As an adult, I came to see that beneath that veneer was a jovial character with a corny sense of humour.

Of a Sunday evening after church, friends would gather in our kitchen where Ray served slice after slice of oven-hot baked bread spread with melting butter and *Koo* apricot jam. Over coffee and bread, seated at the table, Ted would hold court in the raucous kitchen. When he was ready to deliver his jokes and had a hard time getting everyone's attention, he'd say,

"Okay, listen...listen now..."

"*Luister nou!*" He would tap the table with his stubby forefinger.

When he finally got a captured audience, his chubby brown cheeks glistened and his eyes laughed as he started into his joke. When they got too long-winded and his listeners started chatting again, having lost interest, Ted would stop in mid-joke and declare,

"*Wag nou*, wait now, I'm still telling the joke, man!"

I'm told by those close to me that I've inherited Ted's corny sense of humour invariably met with the rolling of their eyes.

Chapter 23

School Days

The transition from *Elnor Laerskool* to Kenmere Primary in Kensington was a bright light in my move home. I adored my standard three teacher, Mrs. Ensel. She was a classy lady who spoke eloquent English in soothing tones. She was kind and I wished she were my mother.

I settled in well and even if I say it myself I think I was fairly popular in the playground.

Outside the humdrum reading, writing, arithmetic routine, there was netball for the girls and soccer for the boys.

But what we girls really prized was being on the Scholar Patrol - *Skollie Patrollie*, jealous kids would derogatively call it. I absolutely swelled with pride when I was invited to join the Scholar Patrol, a prestigious position open only to final year pupils who were scholastically at the top of their class. We had elite status in that we wore special paraphernalia, and got to leave class thirty minutes earlier than the rest. We didn't need to ask permission to leave, even if the teacher was still busy with her lesson. We could just get up and go.

Now we didn't just saunter down to the curb with our stop-sign poles. No siree, we were a fine-tuned five-girl brigade who took great pride in our positions. Decked out in navy blue berets, white military style sashes with badges, we'd get into formation at the gate, make an about turn, and start marking time. When Maureen Ross, our captain blew her whistle, off we'd march, left, right, left right…along the sidewalk to our designated patrol spots. If I felt powerful making cars stop, I can only imagine how heady Maureen must have felt. Come to think of it, she did have a way of strutting around the school yard like a pudgy little bantam hen.

I liked my time at Kenmere Primary and was sad when those days came to an end. I was apprehensive about the thought of high school, going from being a big fish in a small pond to a minnow in an ocean. And I'd seen the high school kids – they were big and looked menacing.

If there was any place forgettable for me, it was Windermere High School. Not only was it an eyesore, sitting on an unkempt, wind-swept, scrubby field, resembling a penal institution, but it was also a place of no inspiration. There was no sense of this being the launching pad for greater things to come in both knowledge and life.

Clad in pleated grey skirts and hideous blazers, Cathy and I walked the mile or so together come rain or shine. We always made sure we got there before the clanging of the old fashioned school bell quietened the schoolyard cacophony, calling us to line up in the quadrangle according to grades.

"Let us pray," Mr Stevens would bellow. He was our principle – "Pops" to us. His nickname was more to do with his age rather than a term of endearment. Pops was somewhat of a contrast to me. On the one hand, he fitted the headmaster bill – an austere, unsmiling individual. On the other hand, he resembled a caricature – balloon belly atop matchstick legs and flabby lips concealing toothless gums. There was talk of his being partial to his tipple.

However, he did have a sense of humour. I remember one morning, Pops standing in his usual spot on the breezeway, facing a rather noisy pubescent throng. "C…a…l…m down, c…a…l…m down," he trumpeted. "Let us pray," he intoned loudly in priestly air.

"Our Father…" We students followed along in discordant mutterings.

When we got to "Thy kingdom come, thy will be done,"
Mr. Stevens yelled, "St…o…p! St…o…p! Don't confuse God
so early in the morning." We got it right the second time.

Sad to say, such light-hearted moments were overshadowed
by darker incidents – corporal punishment and molestation.
The cane was an integral part of our school culture. If you
spoke when silence was expected, you got the cane. If you
performed badly in a test, you got the cane. If you failed to
turn in homework, you got the cane. If you broke the rules
in any way, you got the cane. The cane and never questioning
authority went hand in glove at Windermere High. Little
wonder I despised most of my teachers. *Klipkop* (stone head)
being one of them.

Mr Stone was running late. The classroom was like a
buzzing beehive - noise and commotion coming from all
quarters. Cathy looked at her watch. "It's half past, he's not
coming."

"Ja, a *lekker* free period first thing in the morning,"
declared another girl.

"No, I'd rather have a free period in the afternoon. Then
we can go home early," I chimed in.

Suddenly, Mr Stone, our Afrikaans teacher, stormed
through the door.

"Hou julle bekke, varke." (Shut up, pigs) *"Staan op,"*
he barked, grabbing the thin bamboo cane resting on the
blackboard's chalk ledge.

We leapt to our feet obediently. With raised cane in hand
he stormed over to me at the head of the row. I stiffened,
looked him in the eye, and held out my hand. It came
whistling down onto the tender part of my palm sending
shockwaves of pain through my body. And then another, and
another. I stopped counting beyond the third stroke. Mr
Stone took sadistic delight watching my flushed face fight
back the tears. For whatever reason, he chose me to be the
scapegoat, for the rest of the class came off Scot free.

"Sit down," he shouted to all us telling us to get our books and do the exercises from pages such and such. I bent down over my satchel on the floor, splashing it with tears as I retrieved my text book. I sat back quietly in my seat and opened my book to the page he had barked.

My classmates looked on in stunned silence. If they felt sorry for me they never voiced it and no doubt were relieved that I had taken the rap. Worse than the physical pain was the injustice of being singled out and knowing that lodging a complaint was futile. A trip to the principal's office invariably ended in further punishment or, at worst, expulsion. 'Rights' was not a word in any non-white person's vocabulary.

Unfortunately, or should I perhaps say fortunately, I can never recall my flag-waving martyrdom without being reminded of an injustice I once inflicted on one of my classmates. I was in standard six at the time. I had forgotten I had loaned my exercise book to Andries. Later, when I couldn't find it, I complained to the teacher who had everyone check their desks. Poor Andries timidly held up the book without saying a word. Out came the ever-present cane. Five cuts later and a burning bum, returning to his desk, Andries looked at me through pained, accusing eyes. I knew I should have spoken up, but I kept quiet. The saying, 'what goes around comes around' proved prophetically true.

Mention math to me and my brain shuts down. Mention Mr Jochems to me, and my insides cringe. That reptilian creature with kinky hair and beady eyes was my math and science teacher for two years. He was obnoxious, lecherous, and spiteful; and I loathed him. It was math class. He was pacing up and down the rows while we were bent over our desks working out some problems. He stopped at my desk. "Go water the beans in the lab for me." So I obediently headed to the laboratory where we were growing beans as part of a science project. Little did I know the plot that lay behind that command.

While watering the plants, I was startled when Jochems entered. In one swift motion, putting one hand behind my back the other behind my head, he yanked me forward pressing his lips hard against mine. His breath smelled fetid as he tried to prise my lips open with his snaky tongue. The gold teeth in his dentures gave off a nasty metallic taste. His mouth muffled my terrified attempt to cry out as I squirmed frantically escaping his embrace and dashing back to the classroom. My legs were shaking as I sat back in my desk trying my best to be as nonchalant as possible. I daren't look up. I was convinced everyone was staring at me and if I caught someone's eye, they would give me a knowing look filled with judgement. I was squirming inside with embarrassment and degradation. I hated my life. Why did such things keep happening to me? My trust in authority was absolutely shattered.

I *heard* Jochems rather than saw him come back into the classroom. After what seemed an eternity, I plucked up the courage to take a quick peek. He was standing in front of the chalk board, hands in pockets, looking generally bored. As the day wore on, my shock and embarrassment turned into internal anger and humiliation compounded by the fact that I once again knew that complaining would be a waste of time. As friendships grew closer, so we girls opened up more to one another. I found out I was by no means Jochems' first victim. In South Africa's paternalistic and sexist society, the adult reaction would inevitably be that the young girl was "asking for it."

Had I understood the government's grand design, I might have realised my school life was no more than to be expected. And had I understood my parents generation's lack of interest in their children's education, I might have realised it was no more than to be expected. But what would a fourteen year old know about such things. Looking back I don't know what ultimately made my school life worse – these instances of injustice and humiliation or the substandard educational system foisted on us by the white government.

Hendrik Verwoerd, one of apartheid's chief architects stated that with regard to The Bantu Education Act, "its aim was to prevent Africans receiving an education that would lead them to aspire to positions they wouldn't be allowed to hold in society. Instead Africans were to receive an education designed to provide them with skills to serve their own people in the homelands or to work in labouring jobs under whites." Besides the obvious degradation, its absurdity is borne out in its logical interpretation spelled out in a commentator's article, "that a black construction worker could hammer nails into planks with the front of the hammer, but could not use its claw to extract nails because that was considered more refined work reserved for Coloured and White artisans."

Fortunately for us, Coloureds' education was a rung up from Blacks,' but still left much to be desired. The Education Act enforced separation of races in all educational institutions allowing the government to maintain control of who received what level of schooling and training. As we were designated to be the factory workers, artisans and office hands in the employment spectrum, so we were provided only sufficient educational means to meet those ends. Extra curricula activities or facilities were non-existent.

While Coloured tertiary educational institutions existed, the opportunities for graduates were again limited, this time by Job Reservation Act, another pillar of apartheid. This kept all the best jobs exclusively for Whites. So, for those who did pursue degrees they did so knowing that they may well would have to leave the country to fulfil their ambitions. Furthermore, courses offered at non-white universities were limited and the standards were nowhere near as high as their white university counterparts.

Little wonder most of our teachers lacked enthusiasm. The situation was exacerbated by the Coloured parental mentality

Mama Whitman in her "Queen
Mother" hat

Mama and I going to town

Papa Whitman

Mama in her hay day

Mama with baby Robert

Ray and Ted's Wedding Day

Auntie Albe in one of
Mama's creations

Auntie Una in a
dress that Mama
made

Ray and Una at Pastor Valentine's
wedding where they sang a duet

Mama and Auntie Minnie

Connie, Gracie and
Jennifer in our Sunday
School clothes

Jennifer, flower girl for
Auntie Rose (Ted's sister)

Jennifer flower girl for another Auntie
with Auntie Albe on the right as
bridesmaid

Papa and Mama Paulse

Mama and Papa Whitman

Uncle Jonathan with
Robert and Ray

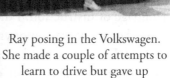

Ray posing in the Volkswagen.
She made a couple of attempts to
learn to drive but gave up

Ray with Sharon (L) and
Jennifer (R)

of the time - pushing their children into the workforce as soon as possible to bring money into the household. Most of us realised that was our fate and consequently made little effort scholastically. For a kid like me who had ability and smarts, wanting more out of life, wanting to break the mould, school was highly frustrating.

The few teachers who did have some spark, who were encouraged by ambitious students, could only lament when a top of the class pupil wasn't there for the start of the new term. Most of us made it to Standard Eight by sixteen, where a pass would earn you a Junior Certificate, enough to equip you for an office job rather than the factory floor. The few parents with foresight encouraged their children to matriculate, giving them the chance of a better job or possibly going on to university.

Windermere High was a typical example of Coloured education fitting the government's decreed template - Afrikaans, mathematics, general science, accountancy, typing for girls and woodwork for boys. That was it. We'd never even heard of extracurricular courses or activities. Option was not a word in our school vocabulary. Afrikaans was the main language of instruction. I didn't like it then and I don't like it now. For me it was synonymous with the oppressor.

Standard Eight was my last school year. I would have loved to have matriculated and gone on to university, but my parents didn't deem education important enough. With eight mouths to feed, you know exactly what I was going to be doing next. My final exam for my Junior Certificate, in November 1972, was a bitter sweet moment for me. I was glad to be leaving Windermere High, but deep down there was a thirst for further education. I knew enough to realise that wasn't going to happen. My best option was to find a job that would ultimately elevate me into a well-paid position.

Chapter 24

Highams

Ronnie Burns, our friend and neighbour from my childhood days in Vasco got me my first job. It didn't take me too long to realise that being a microfilm operator was not the stairway to an illustrious career. So I started scouring the weekend classified ads in our local papers. *Debtors Accounts Clerk – duties to include, typing, accountancy and data preparation. Apply in writing.* Typing and accountancy – that sounded much more up my street and what's more it was on a regular bus route. Oh, the thrill of receiving good news in the mail a week later; I had an interview date.

Leaving home, I brimmed with confidence. By the time I got off the bus my stomach had turned into a cement mixer. I found the place easily enough - Highams (Pty) Ltd. Climbing the dank, dark stairwell to the second floor wasn't too encouraging – not exactly the fancy plate-glass building I was hoping for.

"I have an interview with Mr. Firth," I told the receptionist.

"I'm Monica," she said amicably, as she cast an appraising eye over me.

An energetic, ruddy, bespectacled man, appeared in the doorway and mumbled something about stepping into his office. I was all set to present my spiel, but the moment he opened his mouth, I knew I was doomed. I could barely understand a word he was saying. What sort of accent was this? Somehow or another, I got to the point where I was shepherded into the office of a no-nonsense, matron in a tweed skirt and sensible shoes. Miss Moore gave me a gap-toothed half smile. At my very best I could manage sixty words per minute, but today, my fingers acted like they had never been on a keyboard before.

Argh! Utter disaster, as I made my way down to street level. Well, at least I still had my job at Micrographix. It came as a bolt out of the blue when I got a letter from Highams the next week offering me the job. And little did I know of the monumental changes this would bring into my life.

I settled in reasonably quickly, encountering the normal hiccups any newbie would. Monica and Eleanor with whom I shared the office made me feel welcome. One of my tasks involved sending form letters to clients reminding them of their overdue accounts. What a sense of power it gave me, an eighteen year old, to put my signature to the letters – *"pay within 30 days, or else!"* I was also responsible for daily banking cheques and cash. For security reasons, as women we never went to the bank alone, even though it was straight across the street from us. Miss Moore usually came with me.

I had been at Highams for about three weeks when I heard Monica's high-pitched voice declare, "Good morning, Michael." An open-faced guy with neck-length brown hair, sporting fashionable sideburns, poked his head into our office. He was short in stature and wore lavender jeans with a V-neck navy blue sweater. "Morning Monica," he said politely. I looked up and caught the gaze of his soft hazel eyes. Monica introduced us. "Pleased to meet you," I put forth. Michael said likewise. After he disappeared to the office next door, out of curiosity, I asked Monica who he was. She mouthed that he was Mr. Graham's son. "Oh," I said matter-of-factly, making an indifferent grimace, giving no more thought to Mr. Graham Junior as I returned to my task. Mr. Graham Senior was the big boss. He put in an appearance two or three times a week and never stayed for more than a few hours at a time.

I saw Michael from time to time when he came down the hall, poking his head into our office to see if Monica had any messages for him. Then he'd disappear through the doorway to the adjacent office that he shared with Edith Moore. He used his father' desk since his dad was so seldom there. Several weeks later, with my documents and cash all set for the bank, I popped in Miss Moore's office. "Bank's closing at one today, Miss Moore," I reminded her. For whatever reason, banks closed at one o'clock on Wednesdays in South Africa.

Looking up from her paperwork, she said "I'm frightfully busy at the moment."

"Michael, do you think you could go with Jenny to the bank?"

"Sure," he offered obligingly, "Whenever you're ready." Michael initiated idle conversation as we waited for traffic to clear to cross the road. Michael was incredibly unassuming and never gave the impression that he was the boss' son.

It was the middle of winter. I had been at Highams about three months. I came down with a brutal headache and a throat that felt like I had swallowed broken glass. I'm sure I looked as bad as I felt. Mr. Firth gave me permission to leave early. On my way out, I bumped into Michael in the hallway. Seeing my pitiful state, he remarked, "You must go home and dose yourself and take care of that cold." I felt he said it with such compassion that I was taken aback. I went home and took his advice and took the next day off. On Monday morning back at the office, he asked,

"How are you?"

"Much better," I replied.

"Well, you certainly look much better."

It wasn't the "how are you?" that struck a chord, it was the caring way and genuineness that he showed. Wow, this wasn't the world I was used to. I came from a dog eat dog environment. If you were down, get over it. Something stirred within. On the bus home, I mulled over this encounter and couldn't stop thinking about this wonderful, owner of the lavender pants.

About three weeks later, on a Saturday afternoon my friend Sheryl invited me along to visit her brother and his family who lived in a suburb near the city centre. I had befriended Sheryl the previous summer when we took our driving tests together. We hung out from time to time -shopping, going to the beach, and talking about work and boys. Sheryl had supported me when I told her about my job change and rejoiced when I landed the position at Highams. As she shifted the Datsun into gear I told her about this guy at work that I think I was falling for.

"But he's white," I said sheepishly. Sheryl's mischievous eyes danced with glee.

"Reely? Get outta here!" she exclaimed, dropping her jaw.

I nodded. "Does he know?" she quizzed. I shook my head from side to side.

"Phone him and tell him," she egged me on impishly.

"Are you mad? Tell him what?"

"Tell him you're a secret admirer."

"What? You're crazy!" I laughed.

Sheryl pulled up at a public phone booth in the main road.

"Come onnn!" she coerced.

Giggling, we squeezed into the stuffy, urine-smelling booth. Cracking open the directory, Sheryl asked what his name was. She ran her finger down the G's.

"Here's a Graham in Bishopscourt," she exclaimed excitedly. "Do you think it's this one?"

"I think so," I replied, uncertainly.

"Go on, dial the number."

"Do you think I should?"

"Go on, don't be a big chicken!" Sheryl's onyx eyes sparkled in her round brown face.

"What do I say?"

"Just say that you want to tell him that you're his secret admirer."

"Then what?"

"Wait to see what he says."

I rose to the challenge, lifted the receiver and dialled. A woman's voice answered and I quickly jammed the coin in the slot. "Hello," I put forth my poshest accent, "May I please speak to Michael?" "Yes. Hold on," she said in a naturally posh English accent.

I grabbed on to Sheryl's arm, my heart beating so wildly it felt like it would leap out of my mouth if I uttered another word. Sheryl's mischievous eyes glowed, eagerly wanting to know what was happening.

"I think it's his mother! She's going to get him," I whispered excitedly, holding my hand over the mouthpiece.

"Hello?" I heard Michael's voice in the earpiece.

"Hello, I'm just calling to tell you that I'm a secret admirer of yours," I blurted.

There was silence on the line.

"Oh yes?" he finally replied, sounding like he was interested in what I had to say next.

I don't recall the details of the brief conversation that followed, but he asked if we could meet. I was completely taken aback, I really didn't know what to expect. I thought at worst he would tell me to get lost and hang up.

"He wants to see me," I mouthed the words to Sheryl who was beaming and hanging onto my every word.

"Where?" I repeated the question that was asked of me, looking at Sheryl for guidance.

"Kloof Nek Road," she whispered, "By the bus stop just before the circle!"

I repeated the information into the mouthpiece. He asked me what time and I asked if eight o'clock was all right.

"Okay then. See you then. Bye," I said. I placed the receiver onto its cradle. Squealing with delight we flung our arms around each other. We stumbled out of the booth giddy with silliness.

I suppose in today's world, something like this would fall under the umbrella of "stalking."

But back then life was simpler and we were in many respects naïve to the ways of the world. The concept of stalking someone was in no one's vocabulary. Sheryl and my behaviour would merely have been regarded as high jinks between two silly friends.

It wasn't exactly business as usual for me at work. I tried to act casually whenever I saw Michael and wondered if he knew it was I. I chirped away excitedly all week, willing the time to pass. Saturday finally arrived, I had the alibi I needed. I asked Sharon and Connie, if they were keen to visit Uncle Jonathan and his family in Elsies River. I knew they'd be game to go rather than spend a Saturday evening at home. Apart from Sheryl, I hadn't told anyone about my "date." My stomach somersaulted as I drove along chatting distractedly with my sister and cousin. Arriving at Uncle Jonathan's I told Sharon and Connie I had to pick something up from a work mate and that I'd be back shortly.

Off I went toward the national road that led to the mountain. The situation was so surreal. I felt as though I was playing a role in a movie or something. What would he be thinking? Did he have any clue it who it was? Would he even be there? And then the unthinkable happened. To my horror, the car stalled at the traffic lights. I cranked the ignition several times. No joy.

Fortunately, I had the presence of mind to know that I should wait a while so as not to run the battery down. Now stranded in an isolated area, my churning stomach turned into a tangle of knots. I prayed in desperation, "Oh please, dear God, let the engine start!" I turned the key one more time. Miraculously the engine came to life. It was way past eight by now and I was sure Michael was long since gone, had he ever been there in the first place.

In the matter of a moment my world had gone from intrigue and elation to fear and despair. My sole objective now was focused on getting the car to Uncle Jonathan's. All thoughts of Michael had gone out the window. I thought it best to make my way into the lit main drag. "Come on car, keep going. Don't stop. Please, please, don't stop." Thankfully I was now in a populated area, half way to Uncle Jonathan's. I could feel the relief rising, but it was short-lived. The damn car stalled again at a traffic light. I cranked for all it was worth. "Come on, dammit. Start! But the ailing Valiant would not live up to its name.

A Good Samaritan stopped and he and his companion helped me push the car to the nearby Caltex gas station. They offered to drive me home. By now, my world had imploded. My father was surely going to kill me. How was I going to explain why Sharon and Connie were not with me? And how was I going to explain why the car, his pride and joy, was not with me?

As I swung the gate open, I saw my father's face peering from behind his bedroom curtain. "Who was that?" Ted asked, as I walked in the door. "*Waar's my kar?*" he added, before I could answer. I had my story ready, but looking back it had more holes in it than a colander. "We were at Uncle Jonathan's and I needed to return something to my workmate in Woodstock. On my way back to Uncle's, the car stalled and wouldn't start and this nice couple helped me push it to the Caltex there in Goodwood."

"Where's Sharon and Connie then?"

"They're still at Uncle's."

To my relief and surprise Ted appeared to have bought my story. He seemed more perturbed about being inconvenienced at such a late hour than about the car and now also having to go pick up Sharon and Connie at my uncles.

"Ai, I don't feel like going out, man," he sighed.

What a night. From the highs to lows to coming off much lighter than I had expected. I woke the next morning with Michael back on my mind. I felt awful for having stood him up –albeit inadvertently.

I felt that what had happened was God punishing me for my deceit and foolishness and opening the door for me to walk away unscathed. But how could I just forget about this man who had showed me such compassion? And he had wanted to see me. Yes, I could walk through that door but surely not before I had apologized. I called Michael to explain what had happened. He thanked me for calling and to my amazement said he still wanted to see me. We made a date for another time.

I was back on an emotional roller coaster and how on earth was I going to make up a story for the next rendezvous? The car's worn water radiator hose had now been fixed and fortunately for me, the stalling incident was for my father, now a distant memory. Again I had my alibi intact. Surprisingly, I can't remember what story I concocted, but it did involve Sharon and Connie, and obviously it was good enough because my father let me have the car again. This time, I got to Kloof Neck where I spotted Michael's '60s chalky Valiant – a hand-me-down from his grandfather. Nothing like as slick as mine.

I parked my shiny Valiant facing his a few hundred yards away, and flashed my lights. He flashed back. I got out and walked up to his car and climbed in. "Well?" I said, very relieved that we had pulled off the meeting. "Did you know it was me?"

"Yes," he smiled knowingly, "I suspected it was you."

If I were asked then what kind of man I, a hopeless romantic, would have chosen to date, my focus would most probably have centred on the external, choosing someone tall, handsome and a fashionably pressed out. Now that criteria simply didn't matter.

As we drove around the isolated mountain road he said, "So tell me about yourself." And I replied coyly, "What do you want to know?" I went on to give him the sanitized version of my family history. I got home that night without any drama

It never crossed my mind that Michael's motive for fulfilling our date might have been an ego boost or purely sexually motivated. It didn't cross my mind that I might well be inviting abuse. How could I, of all people, in light of the frightening encounters I'd experienced place myself in such a vulnerable position, especially when I'd heard adults say "she was probably asking for it." I was obviously oblivious, woefully naïve and desperately needy to have implicitly trusted this man's motives to be genuine.

Chapter 25

Two Worlds Apart

Picture this. Boy from affluent background, private school education, university degree, member of exclusive social clubs, home in the leafy suburbs. Girl from lower socio economic family, left school at sixteen, works as clerk in factory. What's the likelihood of their having a relationship? Intimacy? – No. Physical? – Could be. But would it last? Unlikely.

Now let me add more brushstrokes to the canvas – the boy hasn't changed. The girl has. She's no longer white like him. She's brown. So what? But look at the backdrop. It's South Africa. Big problem. He's obviously only after the sex and he's playing a dangerous game. That would certainly be the perception given South Africa's complex racial history and laws.

Looming large was the ever present Immorality Act that forbade romantic, sexual relations and marriage between Whites and Non-whites. White South Africa was made up of the English and Dutch decedents - the latter known as Afrikaners. Afrikaners of those days were a staunchly religious people who saw themselves as "Israelites" of this "Promised Land, believing apartheid to be right in the eyes of God based on the Biblical declaration in Deuteronomy that Israelites (God's chosen people) were not to intermarry with pagans. In their case, pagans equated to non-white. In 1948, the National Party came into power and with them the birth of apartheid. The vast majority of Afrikaners were ardent Nationalists.

I was a romantic - a dreamer. I'd been in and out of love before, but this was different. That he was the boss's son didn't matter. That he came from wealth or not was immaterial. That he had a university degree and lived in Bishopscourt meant nothing to me. All I saw was the man and the regard and respect he showed me. I'd never known this before. The political dangers of apartheid were the furthest things from my mind. As our relationship progressed, I never sensed that he was out to take advantage of me. Our liaison had to be clandestine. We couldn't do anything that normal couples could do in public – stroll in the park, go out to dinner or the movies, go to the beach, and so forth. In fact, any contact, however innocent between a young non-white female and white male would immediately raise suspicion. So where did we go? Where could we go? Home? Our parents didn't know about us. It's the last thing we wanted them to know. Sordid as it might seem, our initial months of courtship were spent in the car. But it wasn't like that. Did we have any physical relations? Sure we did. We were after all two normal young people who were strongly attracted to each other.

Boys of my own race tended to be highly egotistic, paternalistic and sexist, interested mainly in self gratification. But here was someone who stimulated my senses and satisfied my thirst for learning. We talked about literature, philosophy and religion as much as I was able to keep up with given my limited education. Strangely enough, of all our discussions we seldom touched on the political powder keg that could blow us out of the water at any moment. I soaked up everything I could learn from him. Michael touched me profoundly when he loaned me a book from his parents' library, titled *Dear and Glorious Physician* by Taylor Caldwell that to this day remains my favourite.

So there we were, socially and educationally poles apart and complete opposites personality-wise. I'm the touchy feely one whereas he perfectly fits the Myers-Briggs IJTP

– Introversion/Judging, Thinking/Perception. Talk about opposites attracting. On the South African social landscape we were the ultimate odd couple.

I'm no psychologist, but looking back, I believe we were drawn to each other out of mutual emotional neediness. I needed someone to love me and vice versa. At one of our secret rendezvous at his house, when his parents were overseas, I happened upon photographs of Michael that rather surprised me. At first I thought the bloated, troubled-looking figure looking back at me was someone else.

"Is this you?" I asked.

He seemed embarrassed that I had seen them. Michael found it incredibly difficult to open up about himself. I knew nothing of his chequered past - of the drinking problem he'd had. It was years later that he felt comfortable for me to probe, albeit to a limited extent, into those painful details.

Michael's drinking began during his boarding school years. He and his mates often skulked out after dark, making a beeline for one of the pubs in town. Bunking out at night carried a heavy penalty that could spell expulsion. So as time was of the essence they chugalugged their drinks down. Michael said he liked the "buzz" and confidence liquor gave him.

He had many friends with a few short-lived flings in between until one girl came along who bowled him over. A few dates later, he declared his love to her, but the feeling wasn't mutual – the classic "I like you, but just as a friend." He was crushed. He explained that he always felt that he was likeable, but not loveable. His buddies seemed to get the 'babes' but he was just good ole Ern (his nickname at school.) He used alcohol to anesthetize himself against rejection and the booze made "good ole Ern" the life of the party.

Friends would pat him on the back reminiscing about this or that wild party and what top form he'd been in. But his recollections of such events were becoming increasingly blurred to the point of his drawing complete blanks as to his even being at some of them. It was obvious from those photos that alcohol was taking him down a slippery slope. He said he should have learned his lesson after wrapping his car around a tree when returning home from the Country Club after a standard night of drinking. To this day he doesn't know how he got home. He suffered a broken collar bone and bruises. He made half-hearted attempts to cut down on his consumption, but soon reverted to his old binge-drinking habits.

It took a second major incident to once and for all sober him up. Off on an ostensible camping trip, about 200 kilometres outside Cape Town, the guys were drinking at a watering hole in the *dorp* nearby. Driving back to the campsite, a police officer pulled Michael over for suspected drunk driving. He was hauled off to the police station where a doctor was summoned to draw blood and perform a sobriety test. He spent the night locked up in a cell. His friends bailed him out the next morning.

A week or so later, the blood test results became available and Michael was duly charged with driving under the influence of alcohol. In court, his lawyer argued that the blood test analysis was obviously faulty based on the attending doctor's testimony that he had performed the sobriety test satisfactorily – walking the straight line, touching his nose and so forth. The physician went on to say that in his opinion, anybody with a blood alcohol level that high would have been comatose. The presiding judge concluded that although the doctor's findings conflicted with the police report and blood analysis, he could not categorically find Michael guilty. In those days a doctor's opinion carried a lot of clout. Michael got off on a technicality.

He was twenty six years old and his life was spinning out of control. His weight had ballooned and his health had begun to suffer. After the court case, being a pragmatist, he seriously took stock of recent events in his life. He recognized that he was not able to cut down on booze – it was all or nothing. While he escaped the penalty he should have paid, the end result was achieved in that he called a truce with drinking. He had a remarkable resolve to be able to do just that – go cold turkey. He said he had done the same with smoking – simply quit. He still went to the club to socialize with his friends, but remained resolute in sticking to his tipple of choice - Cocoa Cola, which it still is today - only now, it's Diet Coke.

Chapter 26

Guess Who Came To Dinner

At work, we found it increasingly difficult to keep our relationship under wraps. We stole furtive glances at each other and secret moments together whenever we could. Our only form of communication was through notes. One day, Michael brought down a basket of invoices from the factory upstairs. He had snuck in a note for me.

> *My darling, my folks are out of town, and I wonder if you could possibly join me tomorrow evening for supper. If you can't I'll understand, although I desperately hope you'll say yes. Would you let me know by tomorrow morning so that I can make the necessary arrangements? Je t'aime, Au revoir,*
>
> *Michael.*

Filled with immense joy and anticipation I quickly slipped the note into my handbag. I could barely concentrate on my work. I got word back to him that it was a yes.

The following day, I wore my blue corduroy, fashionable maxi pinafore and black boots to the office.

"Oh, you all dressed up today," Monica observed.

"Yes, I'm going out after work to friends' for supper."

"Where do your friends live?" quizzed Eleanor, ever nosy.

"In Walmer Estate," I lied.

"Oh, that's nice," she said.

I couldn't wait for the day to end. Michael picked me up at our pre-arranged spot. I had no idea where he lived or what to expect. All I cared about was being with him, nothing else mattered.

We drove through the leafy suburbs on the road with the yellow streetlights. I remember travelling on this main thoroughfare when I was a child and struck by the pretty yellow lights and registered that this was where the rich white people lived. The car climbed up the road past the Kirstenbosch Botanical Gardens, where my family came during holidays for special outings.

Michael's neighbourhood was a world away from Kensington. Bishopscourt boasted avenues redolent with lavish homes, gardens and gorgeous vistas. Our house had a number, but theirs had a name – *Claverhouse* – eponymous of the branch of their ancestral Graham clan of Scotland.

A Swiss cowbell clattered as Michael opened the solid wood front door. Wow! The entrance hall was bigger than my bedroom, I'd seen such a staircase in films only. It was surreal for me to be walking on Persian rugs and being surrounded by original paintings, fine china and gleaming silver. And the bookcases stacked with volumes. I stood in awe. To me, this was a veritable palace.

As I admired art pieces and sculptures, my eyes were drawn to portraits on the mantle of a pretty, fresh-faced woman. I asked Michael who it was.

"It's my sister, Judith," he replied matter-of-factly. "She was killed in a car accident several years ago."

"Oh, I'm really sorry," I said, genuinely feeling a pang of emotion. He didn't say any more about his sister and I was too much in awe of my novel surroundings and this incredible experience to press for any details.

"Why don't we go through to the study for drinks?" He led the way.

The study! Wow - like being in a movie. Before fixing the drinks Michael struck a match to the kindling in the hearth.

"What kind of music do you like?" he asked, handing me a stack of vinyl LPs.

Shuffling through the pile, I pulled out The Seekers. "Oh play this one please," *I'll Never Find Another You*. I know this probably sounds like something from a mushy movie script, but this is exactly how it was for me. I wanted someone to pinch me to know that I was not dreaming. I wish I could write that there we were sipping champagne by the roaring fire, but Michael being a teetotaller and my not drinking, it was *Schweppes* sparkling bitter lemon. But for the moment it was right up there with be *Dom Perignon*, for all I cared.

The dinner bell tinkled. We made our way to the formal dining room with its polished solid teak table surrounded by twelve elegant chairs. Through the bay window the suburbs down below sparkled and twinkled beneath a canopy of navy blue sky. Cape Town looked so magical and benign from this vantage. Victoria, the Xhosa domestic servant and cook, clad in her utility pink uniform served us dinner. I shall never forget this meal for as long as I live. T-bone steak with baked jacketed potatoes, cauliflower with cheese sauce, and green beans. This was the first time I had ever had T-bone steak. It was unbelievable.

When we were done, Michael sounded the brass bell. Victoria came through on cue and quietly collected our plates. "Thank you, Victoria, that was superb," he said. She smiled shyly. I daintily dabbed the sides of my mouth on the crisp linen napkin as if I did this every day! Thank goodness for the table manners Mama had taught me. I'm sure I would have done her proud. Victoria reappeared with a mouth-watering baked lemon sponge pudding served hot with vanilla ice cream - Michael's favourite. This was another new dish for me, and now one of my favourites.

One of Michael's endearing qualities is his wonderfully unassuming manner. He never felt the need to talk about his parents' wealth or their high society friends. He didn't tell me much about his family background. It's only over later years that I learned that I had dined at the same table where well-known members of Cape Town society - leading judges, businessmen, and academics enjoyed Nancy and Jesse's hospitality.

I had seen in period movies how aristocrats "repaired" to the study for coffee, liqueurs and cigars. We did more than just repair to the study. With the music playing softly in the background, we settled on the rug staring at the fire. Michael gently pulled me down and kissed me tenderly. I could feel his heart pounding wildly against my chest. We abandoned ourselves in raptures of intimacy and passion in "a world of our own." I wished the magic could last forever. And to think in the eyes of the law such a precious moment was completely illegal and could land us in prison. Oh what night!

Chapter 27

Sibasa

The company name Sibasa Trading Store on invoices and statements periodically crossed my desk. At the time it meant nothing to me. But as I got to know Michael better, I learned Sibasa was an important part of his boyhood. This is where his roots began, thirteen hundred miles north of Cape Town. I had no frame of reference as to where in the world Sibasa was. It seemed to me as foreign as Timbuktu.

Sibasa was a dot on the map, not far from the Kruger National Park, in the heart of the Venda and Shangaan tribal homeland. Michael's grandfather, Horace (Billy) Graham who emigrated from poverty-stricken northern England at the beginning of the twentieth century acquired the trading store. Michael's father and uncle ran the business when Horace retired.

It supplied the locals with everything from groceries to blankets. Over the years it expanded - post office, gas station, bank and wood furniture workshop were added – all run by the Grahams. It was a veritable 'Grahamsville' out there in the sticks. Michael talks nostalgically of times spent in their first home there with its deep veranda surrounded by mosquito gauze and polished cement floor, large enough for table tennis as well as deck quoits and darts.

Michael was about five when the family moved to Cape Town, but every year they'd go back up to Sibasa for about a month for the annual stocktaking. Jesse's brother and his family would also come up from Johannesburg.

Most evenings were spent play rousing tournaments on the veranda, the competition was always fierce.

Michael has fond memories of the heavens periodically opening, machine-gunning giant-sized raindrops on top of the *sinkdak* roof creating such a racket that everyone had to shout to be heard. The children loved this and exaggerated the shouting.

But what really stands out for him about Sibasa is his *kakbalie* experience. (Fancy us having that in common!) He said out there in the jungle doing your ablutions was no mean feat. For one, you'd better make sure you got your business done before dark set in. And you never just casually entered the outhouse door. You gingerly prodded it open with the pole, a permanent fixture leaning against the wall, to check that it wasn't 'engaged.' You wouldn't want to accidentally step on a black or green mamba, among the world's most venomous snakes, curled up in front of the long-drop commode. Reptiles notwithstanding, my 'Tarzan' lived in the real jungle with real jungle sounds - lions roaring, elephants trumpeting and the like. A visit to the loo was definitely not to be taken lightly, you never knew what you could run into.

Michael's brother, Roger, told me that for the Graham children, Sibasa was the most African experience they would ever have. He describes the region as "paradisiacal with aromatic smells, lazy temperatures, enormous tropical fruits, slow rhythms and ever-present colours of beauty –where time seemed irrelevant. It was a place without a care in the world, waiting to be explored by young boys. It was a place where we could be naughty and get as dirty as the red dust could make us."

This was the Africa I didn't know – the cacophony of wild life cries throughout the sultry nights mingling with the thudding of tribal drums. One of the rituals unique to the Venda's is the *Domba* dance, an occasion celebrating rites of passage of young Venda women into puberty.

Long files of bare-breasted maidens linked at the elbows, performed the *Domba* dance (snake dance) imitating the sinuous movements of a python with remarkable choreography. Venda legend has it that in Lake Fundudzi in the upper Mutale River, lives the giant python god of fertility that demanded the sacrifice of a maiden each year. To Michael's knowledge human sacrifices weren't part of Venda tribal life. The Grahams were privileged to be invited to one of these ceremonies. This was an integral part of Venda tradition and by no means a tourist attraction.

Mention of the Kruger National Park invariably brings to the fore Michael's 'elephant encounter.' He was about twelve years old, when during a stay in Sibasa, the children pestered their parents to go on a day's outing to the game reserve. Because the men were busy with stocktaking, Nancy Graham and Nancy Crossley (an English relative) acquiesced. Nancy Graham drove the forty miles to Punda Milia, the northernmost gate. "We were having a great day," Michael recalls, "spotting all kinds of animals but we certainly not prepared for what lay beyond the bend.'

There around the corner was a herd of elephants crossing the shingled road with mother and babies joined tail-to-trunk. "It was most cute, of course, but the bull elephant that guarded the herd did not think *we* were," Roger remembers. The bull began an aggressive advance on the car. Nancy set the vehicle in reverse and slowly eased back, but as she did, the bull began to charge. She floored the accelerator struggling to keep the car on the road.

The vehicle stalled in the shallow shingle embankment created by road grading. The elephant was relentless. Roger remembers crouching down behind the driver's seat with his eyes firmly closed. Michael's reaction was that of fight or flight. He made a move to open the door on his side, when Nancy Crossley screamed, "Michael! Don't open that door!"

Had he done so, he would surely have been trampled by the angry bull.

From all accounts it was a terrifying experience. The elephant stopped mere inches in front of the car, trumpeting wildly with ears flapping menacingly. "All I could see through the windscreen," Michael recalled, "were these monstrously thick, grey legs." Roger said he kept his eyes tightly shut throughout the whole ordeal. As to Judith's reaction, no one can remember as everyone was caught up in his/her own terror. The elephant began to back away ever so slowly, swaying from side to side, continuously trumpeting. Eventually, having reached the point where his herd had safely crossed, he lumbered off into the bush. Michael said they all sat in paralyzed silence for what seemed forever. His mother was never keen to visit the Park again.

Chapter 28

Judith

My first knowledge of Judith was through her soft, kind eyes and winning smile emanating from photographs on the mantel at *Claverhouse*. I could never get Michael to talk about his sister. My questions were always met with "Sorry, but I really can't remember anything about her birthday, the night of the accident, the funeral or anything.

Other family members recall Judith and her untimely death vividly. Roger recollects, "Monday, 1 November, 1965 – Judith's birthday. I happened to be at boarding school. On the Tuesday, I was called down to the House Master's office (never a happy experience for any boy.) The master's face was somber. He asked me to sit down and told me that my sister had been in an accident and that my parents wanted me to go home. My father was sitting on the bed in Judith's room when he called me in. The scene is fresh in my mind because I'd never seen my father cry before as he broke the news to me that my sister had died."

Over the years, living with Michael I came to understand how his highly logical mind would simply compartmentalize experiences in his life that were too painful to handle. He would lock them away, throw away the key, never to revisit them. "What's the point?" he'd say. "I see no mileage revisiting the past."

I learned that on her birthday, Judith and her boyfriend were returning from a party in the city along the busy stretch of Cape Town's De Waal Drive, a divided highway with cars going at high speeds. Judith had persuaded her inebriated boyfriend who was driving erratically to pull over so that she could take the wheel. When she climbed out of the car, her scarf evidently blew off. In her rush to retrieve it she was struck by a speeding vehicle. Critically injured, she lay in a coma and died four days later. Michael's Aunt Rae Graham said she clearly remembers Michael's reaction to the tragedy. He plainly showed his pain at the funeral. He kept questioning "Why? Why?" His cousin Felicity recalls that not very long after Judith's funeral, their families went camping. At the campfire, Michael broke down and Jesse put his arm around his son leading him away to comfort him. (Michael has no recollection of this.) Felicity said "I remember being taken aback when Michael broke down, because at our times together at Sibasa he always seemed so "together."

Roger said he regrets not being allowed to mourn his sister's death. His parents thought the trauma of the funeral would be too much for their twelve-year-old son. On the day of the funeral Roger competed in a swimming gala, winning the diving competition. "For my parents it may have seemed a positive thing," Roger reflected, "but in hindsight the void it left in my life through not saying goodbye to Judith will never be filled. I'm sorry my parents handled it the way they did, but in the colonial way they kept my emotions at bay and decided to let me get on with my school life and not be caught up in the mourning process. It's hard when you know how much you miss somebody whom you didn't really get to know for the person she was, though you sensed that she was wonderful." Judith's death remains an incomplete chapter in his life, Roger said. The aftermath of her death was deeply felt at *Claverhouse*.

One's twenty first birthday in South African culture was a big deal – the rite of passage into adulthood. For the Graham children it seemed like a bad omen – Judith was killed, Michael had a drinking problem that nearly killed him in a car accident, and Roger came close to losing his sanity zealously embracing a strict form of Transcendental Meditation. The Grahams had seen one tragedy after another. Then years later, people deemed Michael and my relationship another "tragedy."

Chapter 29

Clandestine Liaisons

I look back in amazement at how I coped with it all. Things on the home front weren't exactly peachy and here I was in a clandestine, illegal relationship. But it's probably just as well that I never stopped to analyze things because there likely wouldn't be this story to tell.

How do you keep from loving when you're not supposed to? How do you keep from expressing your love when you're not supposed to? But as the saying goes, where there's a will there's a way. At work Michael and I instinctively found ways to communicate. We said volumes through furtive glances and thank goodness for pen and paper.

Miss Moore unwittingly became a catalyst for our being able to snatch moments to be together. She was quite happy for Michael to accompany me to the bank on a regular basis. This was the highlight of my day where we could speak without raising suspicion. Unlike almost any other young person, I longed for Monday to come and couldn't wait for the weekend to end. Since Michael had a set of keys to the office, he and I got to work earlier than we needed so that we could steal a few intimate moments together. I found great solace in Michael's notes and often read them several times over. Simply running my hand over his handwriting that I'd come to know so well and reading his wonderful romantic prose comforted me immensely.

Hi love,

Having searched in vain for my clip-board on which I intended writing this short work of art, I have had to resort to adopting a more accustomed pose – namely sitting at a desk! I happened to overhear snatches of your teatime conversation (I know, don't say it - it's rude to eavesdrop) concerning pros and cons of moving out of home. Eleanor offers some matronly but probably very sound advice in saying that it's as well not to be too hasty in one's decision.

My mind's somewhat restless right now and full of wild dreams and ideas. I'd like to fly away with you to a Swiss chalet high in the Alps with the snow lying deep all around outside and the two of us all cosy round a beautiful log fire. And slowly we'd learn more about each other and I'm sure grow even fonder of one another. But unfortunately we live in a real and not a dream world.

And my reason for this note? None at all other than enjoying any form of contact I can make with you – i.e. it's just an excuse to perhaps get some sort of reply from you (if I'm lucky) to do my heart and ego good!

(That's word for word what he wrote all those years ago. Yes, I kept those notes.)

Unbeknownst to me, Michael was always working behind the scenes to make it easier for us to see each other without having to skulk around in the dark and always meet in his car. He was excited about securing a two-bedroomed rental cottage that he shared with his friend, Cammie.

Love,

*Missed you very much this weekend. Could you possibly
come home with me after work to our new cottage and
have a bite of supper. If it's okay let me know before
lunch as I'll be taking most of the afternoon off to buy
provisions, etc. and will be back probably shortly before
five. M.*

The cottage, with its postage stamp secluded backyard
was in a built-up White area. So I still had to be extra
careful about not being visible. Michael ordered a take-out
dinner from the nearby Italian restaurant. I watched him
with fascination as he prepared the salad, slicing tomatoes
and cucumbers with his left hand. In my world this was
woman's work. And not only that, but knowing that he came
from a house with servants and a cook, I never imagined
he would've done this sort of thing before. He set the table,
clearly enjoying playing the gracious host. He certainly was
an anomaly where it concerned South African men.

I was unfamiliar with this pasta dish, then popular in
restaurants and in the homes of trendy White people. I had
never been to a restaurant. I don't even know if there were
any restaurants for Non-whites.

Sitting at the small kitchen table, I dished a portion
of lasagne onto my plate and helped myself to salad. After
tasting my first forkful, I exclaimed. "This is delicious…I've
never tasted anything like it before!"

"Really?" Michael replied, "You've never had this at
home?"

"Mm-mm," I mumbled, turning my head from side to
side, being mindful of my manners not to speak with my
mouth full. The tangy tomato and ground beef mixture
sandwiched with soft, creamy cheese sauce between layers of

tender lasagne pasta sheets was one culinary education my taste buds would not soon forget.

This might seem so mundane to many, but for me it was magical. Every step I took I was touching new ground. And an added joy was now we had a place to meet.

Chapter 30

Vettie's Party

My first 'public' encounter with Michael's social set was at Vettie Wilson's party. Vettie (Fatty) was Michael's best mate since their boarding school days at Diocesan College (Bishops). When Michael dropped the bombshell about us, Vettie in his inimitable way, evidently uttered, "What the fuck Ern! I don't know what to say, man. I'm just afraid that if you guys get found out by the law, I mean, you'll be in serious *kak*, you know that, don't you?"

I had first met Vettie at his factory where he ran a wrought iron manufacturing operation. He towered over the two of us like some big blond mythical god when he met us outside the enormous metal sliding door of his factory. He gave me a distracted "Hi" when Michael introduced us and led us to his cluttered make-shift desk. "Excuse the mess, hey," he said gesturing us to sit down in the two chairs in front of it.

"Can I make you guys some tea?" he offered as he plugged in the kettle.

To my recollection the guys talked shop, Michael being interested to know how the business was going. I sat silently observing Vettie's nonchalant attitude as he sucked on his cigarette, talking through a smoky mouth, his blue gaze directed mainly at Michael and then occasionally at me. Once again I was in a novel environment. I had feelings of apprehension mixed with fascination. I hadn't the confidence to enter into the conversation, but felt good that we had an ally in Vettie. I knew Michael wouldn't bring me to an unsafe place. I was out of my comfort zone but nevertheless this all made me feel liberated, grown up and worldly.

I had made the necessary arrangements to have my alibi in place for Vettie's party. I was getting good at this! As far as my parents were concerned, I was going on a weekend camping trip with a group of friends from work. I chose a simple long brown dress that I accessorized with a string of fashionable polished wooden beads – a birthday gift from Michael. I was a tangle of nerves at the prospect of meeting his friends as we drove up the long farm road to Vettie's illuminated house in the country. The bar was set up on the spacious veranda of the sprawling farmhouse manned by half a dozen brown-skinned barmen decked out in white jackets and black slacks. Mine was the only brown face among the sea of merrymaking guests. While mixing and serving drinks, I could see the bartenders stealing quizzical glances at me, as if to say, "Wait a minute, you don't fit into this picture, what are *you* doing here?"

However much Vettie and his wife Annie did to make me feel welcome; I still felt incredibly ill-at-ease. It was like having an 'out of body' experience. I was operating mechanically – my mouth was smiling and saying "how do you do" as Michael introduced me to numerous friends. I felt flushed and dreadfully self-conscious. I imagined that every pair of eyes was boring into me like laser beams and at any moment I would disintegrate.

On the one hand I wanted to be as far away from this place as possible, while on the other, I wanted to be as close as possible to Michael. "Come on, let's dance!" Vettie boomed, grabbing my hand and guiding me onto the crowded veranda cum dance floor. I was glad for my long dress so people wouldn't notice my leaden feet performing clumsy out-of-rhythm steps. Goodness knows what my arms did, but I flashed a friendly smile, inwardly feeling like a tortoise that was just barely daring to peek out of its shell. This incident is without a doubt tops on my 'most -awkward- moments- in-my- life' list.

My very presence at this party was revolutionary stuff – this was against everything apartheid stood for – Whites and Non-whites could never be on an equal footing in any respect – socially, politically, and philosophically. It was perhaps naïve of Michael to want me to meet his friends and vice versa. However self-conscious and odd we both felt, he had wanted me to be socially accepted by his friends. And to their credit most of them tried to make us feel both welcome and included. The musical number faded and Vettie disappeared into the crowd. I went into a momentary mild panic, like a toddler who had lost its parent as my eyes searched for Michael in the subdued light. He found me and asked if I was okay. I smiled and shyly mouthed, "Yes." We mingled a while until we felt too ill-at-ease to stay any longer.

We thanked Vettie for a lovely party and again ran the gauntlet of the brown barmen as we made our way to the car. Michael navigated the old Valiant back along the pitch dark national road to the cottage where we pretended to be a "normal" couple. My mind whirled about the night's experience. He broke the silence. "Sweetheart, I know it wasn't easy, but you handled the situation very well. I was proud to have you with me tonight."

Up till then, as a couple, our social life had been non-existent for obvious reasons. Michael didn't want the party outing to be a one-off experience. So he arranged a movie night at his place, as of course anywhere else was off limits. He rented a movie projector and invited a few friends to the screening of *Bonnie and Clyde*. We prepared nibbles and drinks again endeavouring to act like a "normal" couple playing hosts to their friends. While they were again kind and accepting, the atmosphere was still quite surreal and tense. Playing at being a "normal" couple was clearly an illusion. Who were we kidding? There wasn't a snowball's chance in hell South Africa, under apartheid, would ever accept our union. Just the mere notion of a mixed couple was repugnant to many whites, especially Afrikaners.

It was shortly after the party, that Vettie and Annie invited us to their farmhouse for the day. Bathed in bright sunlight the magnificent landscape of Vettie's several acres of property complete with majestic mountain views was a treat for me. We lounged on comfortable outdoor furniture on the roomy veranda where just a few weeks before we had danced, sipping pre-lunch drinks. The Wilson children were as cute as could be. I got a real kick when Polly their five year old, asked me if my 'husband' and I were coming for a ride in Daddy's boat on the pond. What a beautiful ring that had to my ears - Michael being my husband. Dare I believe in fairy tales?

"Polly darling," Vettie replied to his daughter. "After lunch we must all have a nap, then we'll go in the boat." Guests were expected to take Sunday siestas at the Wilsons', because Vettie directed us to a spacious high-ceilinged room with a big soft bed. The fact that I remember most things to the last detail, was because they were all so completely strange to my world, right down to the gentle way Vettie spoke to his children. I can only describe my experiences in Michael's White world as playing a part in a fantastic film.

Now Annie has always been besotted with poodles. On a recent trip to South Africa, we stayed with Vettie and Annie, this time at a different homestead in the country. Again poodles of all sizes roamed everywhere. Although this time a Great Dane towering over the canines lumbered amongst them, looking quite out of place. Their adult son had apparently left it behind when he moved out.

Annie laid on a scrumptious leg of lamb dinner complete with all the trimmings. We were joined by another of Michael and Vettie's old school day pals and his wife. Seated around the over-sized farmhouse table, where conversation and wine flowed freely, toward the end of our meal, Dougal the smallest poodle jumped up beside Annie onto the bench. And from there up onto the dinner table, right next to the platter of lamb which to my surprise he totally ignored. He sat facing Annie and the two gazed lovingly into each other's eyes. "Yes, I know," cooed Annie as if talking to a baby, "You're not supposed to sit on the table. I know. I know."

Annie must've sensed that I was completely flawed by this display. "Oh," she gushed half looking my way, "He is the love of my life. He was dreadfully ill and we almost lost him, didn't we, didn't we?" And with that she tickled the black ball of fluff behind the ears. English people are stereotypically known for their fanatical devotion to their dogs. Did I mention Annie was English?

Chapter 31

The Immorality Act

Growing up, my education was taught by rote. You were never encouraged to ask questions and if you did, you were branded as being too big for your breeches. So you never questioned your teachers, grownups and God forbid, your government.   So I never questioned why there were signs in the city on benches and public entrances that read, *Slegs blankes* and *Slegs nie-blankes*. I simply did as I was told and used my designated entrance and went with my family to our designated beaches and didn't wander from my designated area.

When I was old enough to read the newspaper, I came across terms like "Coloured Affairs, Group Areas Act and The Immorality Act." I noticed headlines such as "White Professor and Coloured Doctor Charged under the Immorality Act" or "45-Year-Old Police Constable Hangs Himself." I read that the professor and the doctor were given suspended sentences. They subsequently left the country, according to the article. The white police constable was so overcome with humiliation and shame for being found guilty of having sex with a black woman, that he took his own life. Newspapers of the day carried such stories which made for titillating reading given South Africa's racial divide.

As it didn't affect my immediate world, I had no appreciation of the dire implications and devastation this law inflicted on people who had a genuine attraction to each other Now, here I was – nineteen years old, sitting next to

Michael in his car under the overpass – a setting that seemed so cold and seedy; the kind of place conducive to criminal activity. The reality was that in the eyes of the law our liaison was a crime. This was South Africa in 1975 - apartheid in full flight. Our relationship was illegal under The Immorality Act, legislated in 1950 banning sexual relations and marriage between Whites and any Non-white ethnic groups. Those who opposed the apartheid juggernaut simply did not stand a chance.

One solitary politician did try. His name was Sam Khan. When the Bill was put to vote, Khan famously described it as "the immoral offspring of an illicit union between racial superstition and biological ignorance." He remarked that "there was nothing biologically inferior or evil about the offspring of mixed marriages, but that the evil lay in the social pattern that doomed the couple and their offspring to an inferior status that will deprive them of privileges that should be the inherent right of every citizen in the country." His plea fell on deaf ears. He was subsequently expelled from parliament for his Communist leanings.

Ironically, one of the first people convicted of contravening the Act was a Dutch Reformed minister who, in 1950, was caught having sex with his servant in his garage. The errant clergyman was given a suspended sentence. His parishioners, on the other hand, were so outraged they bulldozed the garage to the ground.

Falling in love for Michael and me was as natural as any couple anywhere on earth finding each other attractive and yearning to be with each other. While we knew in our country it was a criminal offence, we somehow mentally dismissed that obstacle. There's a saying that 'love conquers all.' We certainly did not have it in us to "conquer" the law - our love just seemed to generate a strength, and possibly a blindness, that glued us together.

Up to now we had been lucky not to have been caught. We were courting danger, all right - like playing the board game *Battleships*, with the police being the landmines. You never knew where they lurked. They hid in trees with binoculars at the ready, they played "gotcha" with their flashlights blinding unsuspecting couples parked in lover's lanes, and they smashed in doors on midnight raids with their cameras voyeuristically snapping away. They collected underwear and bed sheets as forensic evidence for court where the penalty for this crime could fetch up to seven years imprisonment. Swaggering and arrogantly wielding their power, the South African police would have done Hitler's Gestapo proud in their efforts to keep the White race pure.

There was no grey in apartheid – it was all black or all white. If you tried to circumvent the law by getting married in another country, the moment you set foot on South African soil, you'd be arrested because they did not recognize the marriage. Every tenet of apartheid caused pain and suffering to the nation – not least The Immorality Act.

Chapter 32

Two Worlds Collide

Neither Michael, nor I wished to deceive our parents. Sneaking around, lying and getting deeper and deeper involved in something that could have dire consequences began to take its toll on me. For obvious reasons, we kept our daylight meetings to a minimum, but there comes a time when with all these pressures you just want to say "to hell with it." It was on just such a Sunday afternoon we dared to take a drive into the country. On top of this Michael asked me to drive. We weren't that brazen as to take the main roads and stuck to the byways. Michael was reading the newspaper, partly out of interest and partly for the screen it provided.

I was conscious of how some other motorists did a double take when they saw us. A mixed race woman, driving at that, and a white man sitting beside her. Imagine that! I pulled into a quiet shaded spot. "Michael," I began, "Would you please put your newspaper down, we have to talk." With a heavy heart I told him we really had no future and we should call it quits before something bad happens. Here was the romantic giving the pragmatist a reality check. But the words came from my head, not my heart. Clearly taken aback, Michael responded with urgency,

"No darling, I couldn't bear not seeing you." That's all I wanted to hear.

It was dark when I got home. The rest of the family were at church. Sharon had left notes on my bed and in my closet to warn me that my parents had been looking for me. I had no alibi, and frankly, I was tired of this cloak and dagger existence. I made up my mind to come clean. Everything seemed unusually quiet - no car or dog noises outside. Here I was a few months into this roller coaster love affair and yet again my innards were churning. Heavy-hearted I sat on my bed contemplating what was to come. Would I get a beating and then have questions asked?

Ted wore a dark scowl on his fleshy brown face. "Where have you been?" he glowered at me angrily as he came into the house. Ray in her church-lady flowery hat, chimed in, "And don't say you were with Sheryl's, because we already checked. "You were gone all afternoon and you weren't back in time for church. What's going on with you?" Ted scolded, his pumpkin cheeks moist and shiny from a rousing Pentecostal preaching workout. Somehow the dull ache of foreboding within me gave way to a surge of courage. With a tortured expression I told them that I was seeing a guy who was white. Ted, who was pacing the floor gazed at me without making eye contact. He never could. He always looked over my head. I had a vague awareness of my siblings quietly observing the unfolding drama like the chorus from a Greek tragedy.

"We *knew* as much," Ray declared brazenly, like a detective who had just made a breakthrough.

"Who is he? Is he married? He's using you. I'm not impressed that he's white," Ted's salvo peppered me. His sentiments were valid because more often than not white men took advantage of girls of colour, got them pregnant and then simply walked away. Past masters had after all done it to their slave women hence the existence of the so-called Coloured population.

"He is not married and he's not taking advantage of me. You're judging him before you've even met him," I cried, my face contorted with anxiety and grief.

"You just stop seeing him or I'll inform the police."

Ted may as well have punched me in the stomach with that threat.

Looking back, I can understand his sentiments. His natural reaction would have been that she was making herself vulnerable to be used by a white man and that he would have been a "poor" white at that. There was a sub-class of lower socio-economic White South Africans whose only means of holding down a job was because of their skin colour thanks to The Job Reservation Act. Ten to one Ted's assumptions would have been correct. Even though I knew he was calling my bluff, I was deeply wounded, and hated him more than ever.

Ray's demeanour became surprisingly subdued as she calmly pontificated how we must obey the laws of the land, whether we liked them or not. "But it's the *law* that's immoral and unjust," I protested. "Still, the law is the law - the Bible says we must obey those in authority over us," Ray opined.

Monday started off gloomily with August's wintry wind and threatening rain. I rode the bus to work really down in the dumps. I wrote Michael a note telling him what had transpired. As always he managed to find a way to send me a reply.

Jennifer, (This sounded so serious. He invariably addressed me as Jen)

Being in the frame of mind I am right now I don't think it's worth my while talking to your parents – at least at the present time as I don't think I'll be very clear in my arguments just at the moment. I'm sorry that I've upset your parents so much – I'm very disturbed by your Dad's reaction although I can well understand his feelings. I'm certain he feels that you and I were far more involved physically than what actually transpired. For as far as I'm concerned and I always will be of this opinion, there was nothing at all in our relationship of which one could be ashamed.

Furthermore, what we enjoyed together I think only you and I will ever understand – and I'm afraid that 99% of the people would probably agree with your father in thinking that our association can only throw a bad light on his name. I only hope that you can slowly patch up what is obviously a very great rift between you and your parents. And I can't agree with you when you apologize for getting me into this whole mess – remember you can't do things on your own – as the saying goes 'it takes two to tango – and I was just as much to blame as you were – in fact more so. I would have told you the essence of what I've said above had I gone to the bank with you. However it appears you preferred not to go with me – well I guess that's something I'll have to accept.

(Michael didn't sign the note.)

I felt as if the world was closing in on us. I didn't know what to think or what to do. I cherished the special love I shared with Michael and the thought of losing him was simply unbearable. Young as I was, I just knew I could never know such unconditional love again.

Chapter 33

I Wanna Leave Home

The more my relationship with Michael blossomed and the more I had a taste of his genteel world, the less enamoured I was with my discordant family life. Don't get me wrong it's not as if home life was totally miserable, it was the unpredictability and unresolved conflicts that plagued me.

As with my mother I had no bond with my father. I suppose I really don't know what bond I expected. Yes, I know Mama and Papa were my grandparents, but they were my surrogate parents. And I know Ted and Ray were my biological parents, but to me they were more like aunt and uncle figures. I'd open up to Mama, but emotionally I felt uncomfortable around my parents. Mama was my only safe place. Mama was gentle. Mama was nurturing. She was what I wanted in a mother. While I didn't have any special relationship with Papa, to me he was loving and tender - very different from Ted's brusqueness and seeming indifference.

Life with Michael had opened my eyes to a wider world. He respected me for the person I was. This new exposure magnified the maladjustment of the seven years I had by now spent under my parents' roof. I detested their religious legalism and strict rules – no dancing, no going to cinemas, no smoking, no pants for women, no lipstick, and no make-up. I hated their hypocrisy - the perpetual rowing, sniping, shaming, put downs and negativity, and not practicing what they preached. I hugely resented having to hand over my monthly salary and be doled out a measly allowance from which I had to cover bus fare and clothing.

Some years ago, reminiscing with my brother in Australia, I found out I was not the only one who resented this outmoded family rule. David, my youngest brother, lamented about the tax refund episode he had with Ted. Although the rebate cheque in the mail was addressed to David, Ted recognizing what it was, duly opened the envelope and demanded that my brother cash it and let him have the money.

"No man, Dada," my brother raised his voice, "That envelope was addressed to me. And that's my money! I'm not a child anymore."

"You getting too big for your boots, you are," Ted replied angrily.

But in his heart, no doubt, he knew David was right. One to generally avoid confrontation, and perhaps underneath admiring David for standing up to him, he relented, but not without sending the cheque fluttering in the air. David was twenty four years old at the time.

I desperately needed to get away. My good friend Sheryl put me in touch with a Mrs Warren. She lived in Athlone, some twenty minutes from Kensington. The 'tour' of her home took all of a minute. Pointing to the double bed, she said in a friendly voice, "Well this is my bed."

My heart sank somewhat when I learned that I would have to share the bunk bed in the narrow galley resembling a train compartment, with her daughter, Judy, who was my age. Never mind, I told myself, I'd adapt and besides which, she had a telephone that meant I'd have better access to Michael.

It's not much," Mrs.Warren said wistfully, "but it's home to us."

We agreed that I could move in the following week.

Saturday dawned. My plans were well in place.

"Please," I begged Sharon, "Don't tell Mum and Dad where I'm going. Please promise me you won't."

"I promise," she agreed, looking sad, but entirely sympathetic.

I gave her a letter to give to my parents after I had left.

When the coast was clear I snuck the suitcase into the Valiant's trunk. Being the only licensed driver in the family besides Ted, I became Ray's unofficial chauffeur. Today was a two hour women's meeting at the church - enough of a window for me to unload my suitcase at Mrs. Warrens' and be back at the church to pick Ray up.

Mission accomplished, Ray sat beside me looking out the window distractedly as we headed back to Kensington. We drove in silence as the automatic Valiant cruised smoothly along the open road. "It's now or never," I told myself trying to pluck up the courage to tell Ray I was moving out. My chest felt tight, my breathing shallow and my mouth went as dry as chalk.

"Mum," I croaked, keeping my eyes on the road, "Um...I decided to move out. I...um...I'm going to board somewhere. I found a place."

"What?" she snapped. I stole a nervous glance to see her reaction. I don't know why, but somehow I thought that I'd be able to reason with her and she'd see my point of view.

"I just feel like you don't understand me." I said quietly. "We don't understand each other." I couldn't quite articulate the cauldron of unhappiness brewing within.

"What's this nonsense?" she cried shrilly, her face glowering. "What's this ungratefulness? We try our best to provide you with a good home. No man, you not the only child to consider. There's the rest of the family. Do we fight? Do we drink? Do we brawl like other people? You come from a decent home. We are respectable. No man, I think you just ungrateful and selfish." She was so wound up that she never asked me where I was moving to.

Ray, continued her tirade when we got home. Her face was thunderous as she marched ahead of me into the house.

Ted was standing by the kitchen counter clattering a teaspoon in his mug of tea. He never stirred, he always clattered.

"Go on," snapped Ray, in her inimitable brassy tone, glaring at me wild-eyed. "Tell your father what you told me!"

"What's it now?" Ted asked wearily, turning his face toward us.

"This one wants to move out – she wants to go board," she blurted out, hitch-hiking her thumb toward me, and not allowing me the chance to do what she had just told me. Ted listened passively.

"*Ai*," he said with a sigh.

"What's this all about now?" He asked rhetorically. "Man, I'm tired; I don't have time for all this nonsense." He took his mug of tea and went to settle on his bed with the weekend newspaper. Ted did not like confrontation. He didn't react because he no doubt thought that it was simply a teenage whim on my part. Little did he know I was planning to fly the coop that very afternoon.

I was resolute in my plans. Ray disappeared to her bedroom and stayed there. I was lurking about in the kitchen to gauge the right moment to make my escape. I went into our bedroom, whispered to Sharon that I was leaving and reminded her to give the letter after I was gone.

"Bye, I'll be in touch." I tiptoed into the kitchen and with the coast clear quickly made a dash for the backdoor. I high-tailed it up Ninth Avenue, cutting across the field to the bus terminal.

Sitting in the bus, my mind went in ten different directions. I let out a quiet sigh as I began to mull over the contents of my letter.

Dear Mum and Dad,

I'm writing you this letter as I find it easier to express myself in writing. I am leaving home and am going to

*board somewhere. I feel that you don't understand me.
We don't understand each other. There are things that
bother me that I don't feel I can talk to you about, or
that you'd ever even understand. I've never felt like I
really belong to your family any way. I don't like the
way we constantly argue. I feel restricted. The money
I earn is not even mine. I have to keep begging for bus
fare. I think it's just best that I leave. Just forget about
me.*

Respectfully,

Jenny.

It was late afternoon. I sat on the lower deck of the bus
that strained and groaned along the grimy, detritus-strewn
Fifth Avenue – a far cry from its New York namesake. *Skollies*
were already high from *dagga* and cheap weekend hooch.
Already in a state of anxiety, my heart sank when a gang of
drunken hoodlums boarded the bus and staggered to where
I was sitting. They were loud, red-eyed and menacing. One
plonked himself right beside me blasting me with alcoholic
breath and boozy flirtation. Strangely, I felt more irritated
than afraid. I was preoccupied with my own unfolding
drama. As I instinctively turned my scowling face away from
the thug, he took umbrage and started swearing. My gut
reaction was to fight or flee. I leapt to my feet, rushing to the
driver. "Please let me off, those *skollies* are bothering me," I
told him.

"*He-ey, kom hier!*" one of the gang shouted, while the
others heaped insults on me. My face was flushed, I was highly
embarrassed and annoyed at being singled out and angry that
the rest of the passengers did nothing. "*Laat staanie mense,
man,*" the bus driver made a plaintive plea as he pulled to the

curb to let me off. He knew better not to press the issue or he could become their next victim. *Skollies* could be vicious. For them life was cheap. They thought nothing of sticking a knife into one.

The phrase, "*Laat staanie mense, man,*" brings to mind another *skollie* encounter. It was a Saturday morning, Ray and I were on our way to catch the bus into town. I was about fifteen at the time. As we approached the crowded terminal, while chatting to my mother, I suddenly felt a limp arm being flung over my shoulder. My body froze with shock, together with my voice box. Try as I might, I couldn't utter a sound. The drunken gang of mobsters had engulfed us like a dark cloud.

Ray was unaware of what was happening and kept talking absently-mindedly, looking in the opposite direction. Once aware of my predicament, she sprang into action like a wounded tigress. She whipped off her high heeled shoe. "You get your filthy hands off my daughter, or *ek slaat jou kop vol gatte!*" she hissed, holding the shoe ready to strike. Ray gave them such a tongue lashing that they backed off. "You go crawl into the holes that you came out of," she scolded, her face hard with anger and her eyes bulging. "And you leave decent people alone!"

"*Kom, laat staanie mense, man,*" said one of the gang, prising the drunken *skollie's* arm from my shoulder. They sauntered away in a *dagga*-induced stupor. As we joined the queue, Ray was still seething. "*Verdomde skollies,*" she bristled. With all the people looking on, this was another time in my life that I wished I could just have vaporized there and then. That was the only time I can remember Ray's latent maternal instinct coming to the fore.

I certainly hadn't inherited her feisty nature of choosing fight over flight. Thankfully, I didn't have to wait too long for the next bus. I could hardly wait to get into town where I had arranged to meet Michael. I made my way across the Parade

to King George V's statue – our rendezvous. Stall holders
had packed up and the parade was open to traffic again.
Saturday workers were going home. The late afternoon sun
had segued into dusk and soon the city's night life would
come alive drawing movie goers, diners as well as sailors,
joy riders, pimps and prostitutes. No sooner had I got to
our meeting place than a slimy-looking, pudgy, middle-aged
white man pulled up in his car, leering at me. He rolled down
his window and said seductively, "Hello Sugar. Wanna go for
a ride?" I scowled at him, quickly walking away to where I
felt safer. He cruised off slowly, obviously in search of a more
willing passenger.

I was a jangle of nerves and I prayed Michael would come
soon. What a relief to see the chalky Valiant. I couldn't get
in fast enough. I made no mention of my intrepid journey.
Sensing my tension, he placed a hand on mine.

"Darling, it concerns me to see you're so troubled," he
said, "Are you sure, you're doing the right thing?"

"I'm very sure," I replied. Although I addressed him as
darling or sweetheart in my notes, I was a bit shy using those
endearing terms face to face. "I just can't take it at home
anymore, I'm desperate to get away." I felt comforted by
Michael's care but more especially just to be with him. He
dropped me off at Mrs. Warrens saying he would ring me
later. That first weekend at Mrs. Warren's was so liberating. I
revelled in my new-found freedom and independence. Mrs.
Warren treated me like an adult and made no demands of
me. In fact she was thrilled I would be company for her
daughter, Judy.

It felt strange negotiating my way to work on a new bus
route. I needed to make an earlier start as I had two buses to
catch. From Kensington into town, Table Mountain's iconic
flat top was my constant reference point. From the Athlone
side, the mountain looked very different. But it was still there,
a steadfast landmark. I would happily adapt, I was sure. The

following Saturday I went on a shopping spree enjoying the freedom of being able to manage my own money.

In our community it was rare for adult children to leave home before marriage. I had no friends who lived on their own. It was as much culture as economics that dictated this arrangement. My office mates showed concern when I told them I'd left home. Eleanor offered her usual matronly advice, "You should go back, Jenny. You're still very young and the world is a dangerous place for a young woman on her own." Eleanor and Monica did not know about my clandestine relationship with Michael as yet.

Alas, my freedom was short-lived. Ray and Ted appeared on Mrs. Warren's doorstep while I was preparing lunch. Ted pressed out in his preacher's suit and Ray in her Sunday-best greeted me stiffly. "Hullo," I replied sheepishly, my skin uncomfortably tingling with flushness and guilt consuming me for being caught in blue jeans and on a Sunday, to boot. They had a "word" with Mrs. Warren in the cramped living quarters.

"We are Jennifer's parents. Mrs. Warren, I believe?" Ray put forth in her holier-than-thou church lady persona.

"Yes. Pleased to meet you," my forty-something, mildly spoken landlady replied.

"Mrs. Warren, we just came to set things straight about Jennifer living here with you. We don't understand how you can take her in just like that and not contacting us to hear the full story. We do our best to provide a good home for Jennifer. We are decent people, Mrs. Warren. We don't brawl; we don't drink. She comes from a good Christian home," Ray held forth, with Ted sitting passively; content to let his wife do the bidding. He had done enough talking in the pulpit, and had to go back in the evening to do more of the same.

"Mrs. Paulse," Mrs. Warren interjected. "I took Jennifer in on a temporary basis till she sorted out her personal problems.

"I don't know why she couldn't come to us with her problems. Now she goes to a stranger," Ray's voice was controlled and not its usual shrewish timbre.

"As I said," Mrs. Warren held forth, "I took her in because she was upset, and I just gave her some space to sort herself out."

"There are two sides to a story, Mrs. Warren," Ray rejoined, "And you have just heard Jennifer's side. We've got five other children to consider and we rely on her to help out financially. We all pull together but she wants special treatment. She's just selfish.

Anyway, there's nothing more to be said. We've come to take her home."

So, the matter was settled.

"Come Jennifer, get you stuff together, we taking you home," Ray commanded. And as always, I complied. I sat quietly in the backseat of the blue Valiant, as we drove back to Kensington feeling totally dejected.

Unpacking the suitcase in my bedroom, Sharon told me Ray and Ted had grilled her into revealing my whereabouts. In the kitchen, an apron-clad Ray busied herself with the roast. Seated at the table, it was déjà vu, Ted tapping with his forefinger between his knife and fork in his customarily manner, "*Kom nou, bring'ie kos,*" he grumbled impatiently. "Bring the food!" As I sat down, his chubby cheeks gleamed as he smiled sarcastically, "Bring out the fatted calf, the 'prodi-girl' has returned." Dismissing feelings and making light of problematic situations was the Coloured way. "Get over it." But for me, his quip made me feel insignificant and of little value.

With lunch out of the way, Ray busied herself washing the dishes. Strangely she didn't ask for my help. When everyone had dispersed, she came into my bedroom.

"Okay, let's have your wages," Ray demanded.

"I don't have it. I spent it," I replied, preparing for all hell to break lose.

"You are damn selfish, you know that!" Ray blurted in her characteristic asperity.   How could you do such a thing when you know the family depends on that money, huh?"

"But that's so bloody unfair. It's my money that I earned. I don't want to work for your damned family!" I wanted to say, but didn't have the nerve for fear of getting my teeth knocked out.

Food somehow appeared on the table during the ensuing weeks and the family survived.   Mercifully, the relationship between my parents and me started to improve, my allowance increased slightly, but my keeping my salary was simply non-negotiable. I worked for the family. That was how it worked in the Coloured culture and that was how it would remain.

Chapter 35

The Weird Interview

Maintaining our relationship in secret at work coupled with constantly having to look over our shoulders, was beginning to take its toll. Although I have a sanguine personality, I also possess an element of pragmatism. I decided to take the bull by the horns. I was going to leave Highams. Scouring the classifieds I spotted an ad for "receptionist" (no colour specified) for a business in the city. I phoned to set up an interview. Could I come on Wednesday at six-thirty, the voice offered. I thought it odd to have a job interview so late in the day, but agreed.

Wednesday, six thirty - I pushed open the glass door into the empty reception area. This was definitely much flashier than Highams. Comfortable chairs surrounded a low coffee table that held an assortment of neatly stacked magazines. My guess was that this was a legal or medical office. I saw no typewriter but I could picture myself receiving whoever it was that frequented this place. I waited about five minutes before timidly calling out "Hello."

A slender brown-haired woman appeared, dressed in casual slacks and red woollen sweater. She gave me a perfunctory "hello" and apologized for not having heard me come in.

"I'm here for the job interview for receptionist," I offered.

"Yes …right," she said. Her manner was casual and matter-of-fact. She didn't seem the type who smiled readily.

"Okay...er...this is the reception, of course," she continued, with a slight gesture of hand.

I smiled and said that it was nice.

"Now, if you would come with me, I'll explain a bit more about the job." I followed her down the hall into what looked like a medical treatment room. In the centre was an examination table.

You can imagine my surprise at seeing a grey haired man lying on the table buck naked but for a small white towel covering his genitals. My first impulse was to flee, but as always, I stood there frozen like a deer in the headlights, doing my best to be polite. The woman introduced the prone man as Rick - I think it was Rick.

"Hi there," he responded in what I pegged as an American accent. "Well, let me explain about the job," he began, still in restful repose. I stood there clutching onto my handbag like it was a lifesaving device in a body of deep water. The plain looking woman stood beside me. I felt like we were two medical students studying a specimen.

"Our clients are mainly doctors, lawyers, judges, and important businessmen who come to us for relaxation. The tips to be made are extremely generous – fifty to a hundred rand just from one client," Rick continued, sounding like a salesman. I had a hunch as to where he was going and thought I'd just hear him out and then beat a hasty retreat. I nodded in acknowledgement as he extolled the virtues of keeping Cape Town's judges and lawyers relaxed. Just when I thought the interview was over, he said, "Tracy will give you a demonstration as to what we actually do." I felt the blood rush to my face. I made a mental note of the doorway. My brain was telling me to run, but my feet seemed *Superglued* to the floor.

Tracy poured oil into her palm and began rubbing Rick's tanned, leathery shoulders and working up into his wrinkly neck area. "The work is not hard," Rick continued, all the while sizing up my reaction. "But as I said, the money is good – especially with those tips," all the while Tracy's fingers were kneading his flesh.

"Okay," Rick assured me, "It's really easy. But just so you can get a feel for what you'll be doing, Tracy will let you have a go." His tone made it sound like he was asking me to take a typing test. "Just take your coat off and just relax," said Rick in a soothing tone.

Like a fool, I complied. I hated myself for being so weak and naïve. Tracy handed me the oil and looked on as my fingers gingerly touched Rick's pectoral area sprinkled with sparse grey hair. My reluctant hand touched the dermis before me as though I was touching a piece of offal. *Oh God, what have I got myself into here* I shot up a silent prayer.

"Yeah, that's right, that's right, don't be shy…" coaxed Rick. "You'll get the hang of it real soon." I'll go get us a take-away then," Tracy said. "Can I get you anything, Jennifer?" I was glad to be distracted for a moment from this freaky hands-on interview. I yanked away my hand from Rick's surprisingly cool flesh, as if I had touched a hot stove.

"Oh, no thank you," I replied timidly, "I've got to go. I've got a bus to catch and it's getting dark."

"You sure?" Tracy asked, grabbing her purse making her way through the door.

Go! Get out now! My head told me again.

"Okay," Rick continued calmly. "You're doing great. Now just do a bit of the torso area and the legs. We do the whole body, you see."

I obediently "did" the torso till I got to his pubis. Rick removed the little white towel exposing his floppy, greying genitals. I had an idea where all of what was happening could potentially lead, but all I could do was pray, *Oh God, please don't let this man harm me. I need to get out of here.*

It was about ten minutes or so later, I heard Tracy return, I told Rick that I really should be going. I grabbed my coat

and bag, said a hasty goodbye as I dashed for the door. I
scurried down the deserted, poorly lit street. Office lights
here and there cast a comforting glow as a place to take refuge
should I spy a potential assailant. Nervously, I made my way
to the near- deserted bus terminal. I was so relieved when I
finally got home.

"Why are you so late?" my mother asked, standing by the
stove stirring what looked like *bredie*.

"I just came back from a really strange interview," I said
and then proceeded to recount all the gory details."

"No my child, God was definitely watching over you.
But why do you want to leave Highams?" I gave her a rather
vague reply saying I needed a change. She seemed content to
leave it at that which suited me just fine.

When I returned to work the next day Highams' musty
offices took on a new look. I made no further attempt to seek
another job, especially after Michael's latest letter.

My dearest Jen,

*Before I go much further please excuse the scrawl. I'm
writing in bed it being Sunday night and bed not being
the easiest place to write from. Furthermore I'm afraid
this is not the world's best pencil. I do have a ballpoint
here with me but of late all the letters that have passed
between us which have been written in ballpoint have
conveyed anything but good news. I sound ridiculously
superstitious.*

*Thank you for your phone call yesterday, my angel.
It's always great to hear from you even though you did
sound depressed and somewhat mixed up. It's all very
unfortunate that we happen to live in the only country*

in the world, which legally prohibits you and I (sic) from associating with each other in a manner we would like.

And the last thing in the world I will ever be embarrassed or ashamed about is our relationship. It has been or rather should I say it still is a very decent and for all the problems we've encountered a very understanding union. I'm just sorry it can't be accepted as such. I will always be of the same opinion – that there is nothing remotely disgraceful, or indecent about what we've enjoyed. After all hundreds of thousands of people fall in and out of love everyday – does it make it a sin all of a sudden if it occurs with two people of a slightly different colour? To this I will always say no.

What I'm going to say now is very selfish on my part but I might as well be honest with you rather than put up a pretence. Your suggestion about leaving Highams gave me quite a shock as I've not entertained the thought up to now. Darling I don't want you to do so – not now at least.

For just having you present and being able to know how you're progressing in your general everyday being and your work is a comfort to me. And I think you're sensible and stable enough to realize that letting our hardships affect your health and work will do both of us more harm and will certainly cause me distress.

Fortunately in this respect our daily contact is very little and as such we can both get on without much distrac- tion – however our short moments together are worth a lot to me and I hope to you. As I say love, what I've said above is of a very selfish nature.

Obviously you must make the decision yourself – if you feel that by leaving and in other words not seeing me again it will solve the problem then I'm afraid that will be the best line to take. I know that in the back of my mind I realize this is the safest and ultimately the sanest solution. Yet at the same time I feel that having to do this is like accepting a hiding for a wrong you've never committed. I think I'll end now before I ramble on too much and become repetitive and thoroughly boring.

Au revoir, my sweet.

Michael might have thought he was rambling, but I treasured every word he wrote. I often read his letters several times over.

Chapter 35

The Meeting

Our neighbour, Mr. Gravenorst lived diagonally across from us on Grumman Street. He and his wife Binnie, were polite but kept very much to themselves. Then Binnie died and before long his house came to life in the memorable character of Auntie Freda, no blood relative. And quiet, gentlemanly Mr. Gravenorst became Uncle Chris to us.

Auntie Freda was highly strung. She walked with a purposeful gait, body leaning forward as if straining against the wind. She was neither fat, nor thin. I thought she looked quite romantic when she went down to the corner store, wicker basket in hand reminiscent of some old-fashioned English lady. She wore her salt and pepper wavy hair in a casual bob. The neighbours found her odd and some called her "that crazy lady" behind her back. But I liked Auntie Freda. She was both dramatic and cultured and I developed a good rapport with her.

Her comfy home was a place of refuge when things got on top of me. I could pour out my heart to her. She and Uncle Chris, both keen gardeners, had transformed their home into a cosy cottage complete with ivy covered porch in the front. Their bountiful vegetable garden and fruit trees in the back reminded me of my Vasco days.

"Oh, Pa worked so hard in the garden today," she'd say in her tremulous Katherine Hepburn voice whenever I complimented her on the garden. I loved the way she pronounced the letter 'p' with her upper lip flapping over the lower one resulting in moist 'p' sounds. She always sounded as though on the verge of tears, even when she was laughing. I loved listening to her stories about her late husband, Cluny Brady, with whom she had one grown son, Peter, who lived with her. She was rather holding out that something would develop between Peter and me, but it was not to be.

When I told her about my romance with Michael, she took a keen interest and offered me succour during difficult times. I told her my parents had false preconceived notions about Michael in that they thought he was only using me, that he'd get me pregnant and then walk away. I wanted them to meet Michael. I didn't know how they would react if he came to our house. Auntie Freda's small tragic eyes brightened up. "I have an idea," she offered in her wobbly voice. "Bring him to my place for tea, dear. Then we'll call your mother to come over to meet him." "Oh that's brilliant, Auntie Freda," I replied. Auntie Freda's house would be a warm setting to introduce Michael rather than my parents' chaotic place. We made arrangements for the following Sunday.

Auntie Freda had set a fine table with her best tea service and was beside herself with excitement at meeting Michael. In the background, Uncle Chris quietly observed the unfolding drama. Introductions were made and tea was poured and word must have got back to Ray and Ted, via my sister, Sharon, that I was over at Auntie Freda's with my white boyfriend. Ray sent word back to bring him to our house.

Had I introduced a guy of my own race would've been one thing, but introducing a white guy from the leafy suburbs, given the political and social situation, was quite another. Auntie Freda, clearly in awe of who Michael was and where he came from gushed forth while Michael looking rather nervous said all the right things.

With our "thank you's" done, we crossed the street in silence to One Sixty Six, both no doubt wondering how all this was going to pan out.

My parents and siblings had just come back from church. Michael and I sat on the green faux leather sofa like two nervous patients waiting to be called into the doctor's office.

Ray, still in her church hat, entered the room flashing Michael a friendly smile. She said she was very pleased to meet him and chatted animatedly about the wonderful service they had had and how good the Lord was. Michael nodded politely. I'm sure he felt flushed from the "heat" in his perceived "fiery furnace." We were all ill-at-ease. This was an abnormal situation.

It seemed like Ted was stalling in his bedroom about having to meet the man he threatened to report to the police some weeks earlier.

As Ted appeared in the doorway with Ray still jabbering on, Michael rose extending his hand to Ted. My father smiled stiffly and in as confident a voice he could muster said, "Pleased to meet you, sir." He said it more deferentially than subserviently. He excused himself to change out of his church clothes. I think Ray offered Michael a cup of tea again. It was difficult to be ourselves in this odd situation in a country where our relationship was so taboo. Michael didn't stay long, it had been an emotional day for the two of us, the more so for him. We stole a kiss at the door before as he left. Afterward, Ray and Ted remarked what a fine gentleman he was and that they could see he came from good breeding. He was not the "white trash" they had suspected trying to take advantage of their daughter. We had crossed the Rubicon.

Michael had unequivocally met with my parents' approval and was now welcome at our home. No longer had we to skulk in the shadows although the coast was far from clear for us.

Under South African segregation laws, we all lived in our separate areas. Whites could not enter the Black townships without a necessary permit and Blacks could not even be in the city at all without a pass which had to be carried at all times. Whites could go into the Coloured areas and vice versa, but a White being in a Coloured area with any degree of frequency would certainly raise suspicions. One could only hope that neighbours didn't alert the police.

Thankfully, we had good neighbours.   So although we were still severely restricted publicly, we now we had a place to meet, albeit not very frequently. As my parents got to know Michael, they became very fond of him. Ray was always concerned about everybody being on their best behaviour because "What would Michael think of us?" Given where he came from, she didn't want us to appear *deurmekaar* Coloureds – we were respectable. When she found out that Michael was partial to tomato *bredie*, Ray enjoyed cooking this traditional dish for him and took delight in how he dug in with gusto. "Shame," she'd say, "You wouldn't be eating *bredies* at home, hey?" In her mind she envisaged White people in Bishopscourt eating the best of the best. She couldn't imagine Michael eating *bredies* let alone pens *en pootjie* curry which she was soon to find out was one of his favourites.

My siblings came to grow fond of Michael too. The younger boys were a bit shy, but as soon as Alan found that he and Michael shared a common interest in sport, conversation flowed readily, mostly with Alan peppering Michael with loads of questions in his inimitable wide-eyed manner of earnest engagement. Since in the Paulse house, going to the cinema was verboten (falling under the category of the sin of "worldliness,") my father brought the cinema to us. He would from time to time rent a projector and reels of film that he screened on a white sheet taped onto the kitchen wall. We'd watch a "short," usually Laurel and Hardy followed by the main feature – invariably a Western. At one such showing, Michael blurted out "Oh, *a skop, skiet en donner movie*". "Whoa! Oh my!" Ted exclaimed and everyone laughed because not only were they surprised to hear Michael using an Afrikaans phrase, but the slang *donner*. It's not that *donner* was necessarily a swear word, but it was deemed 'strong language' in polite company.

"What did I say?" Michael asked bewilderedly.

Michael recalls either Ted or Ray answering, "We don't use that word" or something to that effect. He promptly apologized.

He remembers feeling highly embarrassed about his faux pas and thought he had definitely blown it with my parents. He thought my father would not allow me to associate with him based on that. But I realized it wasn't anything like the big deal Michael had perceived it to be.

Now that my parents had put out the welcome mat for Michael, the few times we could meet over the odd weekend, but not being able to go out publicly we spent countless hours playing *Scrabble*! Besides the obvious pleasure it was for me to have Michael come see me at home, it also provided the opportunity for us to experience the cultural exchange that we'd not otherwise have had. Segregation meant that very few neither knew how the other half lived. On our part we saw Whites (other than "poor" Whites) living an ivory tower existence. Conversely, Whites had a stereotypical view of Coloureds sketchy eking out an existence in filthy, shabby dwellings in wind-swept, sandy suburbs. It never occurred to them that behind the cracked facades were some of the best-kept homes, nor did they have the opportunity to experience brown people's generosity and warm hospitality.

Chapter 36

The Jaguar

"Okay, Mr. Castleton, here's the deal. If you haven't come up with the cash by Friday lunchtime, this ticket's all mine."

"Yes, yes, I'll definitely have it when I'm in on Thursday, no problem," Mr. Castleton assured Michael.

"Okay then, but just remember if I don't see the colour of your money, this one's all mine. And you do realise this is the winning ticket I'm holding in my hot little hand."

"Don't you worry," was Mr. Castleton's rejoinder, "You'll have my share before Friday."

This conversation took place not long after our car-chasing encounter. Mrs. Gates, one of the factory managers breezed into our office holding a handful of raffle tickets to raise money for her son's school's sports pavilion. They were much too pricey for us office girls. She went next door where Michael was chatting to Mr. Castleton, one of Higham's sales representatives. I could hear the whole conversation coming from the other side of the wooden partition that divided our downstairs offices. Mr. Castleton said he didn't have any cash on him, so Michael offered to pay the full ticket price.

Thursday came and went – no Mr. Castleton. Friday came and went – still no Mr. Castleton. Later that Friday afternoon, with my head down engrossed in paperwork, I looked up to see Michael approaching my desk holding a basket of invoices that routinely came to me from upstairs. I noticed a piece of notepaper strategically sticking out from the pile and quickly retrieved it. The scrawl read,

Sweetheart, won't you have a bite with me after work?
Please say yes. I'm leaving early to get in some provisions.
I'll pick you up at the bus stop.

Love,

Michael

Dining at Claverhouse (Michael's parents were out of town) the phone rang. Michael excused himself to answer it.

"Good Lord," I heard him say. "Are you sure?"

I heard the receiver click back on its cradle. As he made his way through the doorway, his eyes sparkled and his face broke into a half smile of disbelief.

"I won the Jaguar," he proclaimed with as much excitement as an introverted engineer could muster.

"What?" I exclaimed, "You did?" I couldn't believe my ears as he walked toward me.

"Well," Michael mused, the gears in his brain clearly turning over, "I guess I can trade the car in and that will give us the cash to buy your plane ticket.

I stood up to embrace him.

"I don't know what to say?"

"Say yes you'll come with me."

Before he kissed me, I pulled back and bantered teasingly, "Are you sure you want to give up the Jag for me?"

"Well, since you're giving me the option…on second thoughts…" he replied with a twinkle in his eyes.

Chapter 37

Facing Goliath

With money to pay for my fare now, we began to make plans. Michael came to ask my parents' permission to take me overseas and marry me. He recalls that to be one of the hardest tasks he had ever undertaken. He sat in the armchair closest the front door - perhaps psychologically ready to beat a hasty retreat should my parents have said no. I sat in the opposite corner. An oversized *Delicious Monster* plant sprawled between us like a great, green chaperone, while Ted and Ray waited for Michael's opening salvo.

The awkwardness of the moment was palpable. Like a well-rehearsed valedictorian, he began, "Mr. and Mrs. Paulse," pausing to clear his throat, he continued, "I have asked Jennifer to come with me to England. As you know, the law such as it is makes it impossible for us to have a future together here. I know it's a great sacrifice for her and for you and I'm here to ask your permission to take her with me to England. I will be embarking on further studies in Leeds and Jen felt she would look into taking a secretarial course there. As soon as we find a church we'll get married, of course."

My parents' eyes were fixed on Michael and I could see their demeanour relaxing when they heard the church and marriage part - we would not be living in sin. I was tense and excited all rolled into one. I didn't know if I should be saying anything and for that matter what to say. So, I just sat quietly, full of love and admiration for Michael.

Ray spoke first. "Well, Jennifer is a grown young woman, and it's really up to her."

Ted nodded and smiled awkwardly. "Yes, it's her decision. If she wants to go, we give you our blessing."

Michael and I shot each other a shy smile.

"Thank you, Mr. and Mrs. Paulse, That's very good of you."

"When are you thinking about going then?" Ted asked.

"Well, I need to work out the logistics still. I need to start my studies at the beginning of September - so, probably toward the end of August."

I had never known such indescribable joy. It was almost too much to take in all at once. I was going to get married to my sweetheart, in England, no less! It was definitely a "pinch-me-and-tell-me-it's-real" couple of weeks as we started talking about dates, consulting the Thomas Cook travel agent and going to Van Kalker in Salt River to have my passport photo taken.

I daydreamed about England and how it would be. How was London going to be? This was still before TV had arrived in South Africa and decades before Google. I could only imagine. Wow, that is where the queen lives and I am actually going there! Word got out and my friends and neighbours were happy for me. Overseas travel was very much a novelty then. I thought that since I was going to England, I'd better start practicing my "ps" and "qs" and speak properly, just in case I ran into the queen!

So I modelled myself after the stylish English secretary who worked at my previous place of employment. I took note of her elocution and how she handled herself with poise. It amused my father the way I changed my image from being ultra fashionable into classical style, pulling my hair back and sounding posh like Sarah-Jane.

There was just one thing left to do before we were 'home free.' When I asked Michael if he had told his parents about us, he seemed reticent. He told me he needed to find the opportune time. What I later learned was that having lived in awe of his father's dominating personality, dropping this 'bombshell' on them was something he dreaded. He explained that he never had the kind of rapport with his father where he could just open up about his hopes and dreams. Theirs was more of a business-like relationship where conversations centred on scholastic achievements and later on career and monetary investments. Not only did Jesse have a strong personality, but was also taller in stature than Michael. Approaching his father was something akin to a David and Goliath scenario.

He knew it was best to test the water via his mother. Now Michael is not a 'chapter and verse' kind of guy and I'm not a 'Reader's Digest' kind of gal. So extracting the details of the whole encounter with his parents was an uphill battle for me.

It was Saturday afternoon and Jesse was out golfing for the day. Michael knew he'd find his mom on the veranda, over a cup of tea, working away on the newspaper cryptic crossword. "Mom and I often did the crossword together," Michael recounted wistfully. She said she hadn't expected him for tea, but was glad he was there to help her with a few clues. It was do or die - now was as good a time as any. Michael spilled the beans.

If anything was to going to put a damper on Nancy's finishing her puzzle that day it was what she had just heard. Being of calm disposition and not outwardly given to panic, she said something to the effect of "Good Lord, Michael, whatever possessed you to get yourself entangled with a Coloured girl? Surely you realise that there can be no future in this."

Michael replied, "I know, Mom. That's why I've asked Jen to come with me to England so we can give ourselves a chance."

"I don't think you're thinking clearly and you're not being fair to the girl in encouraging such a relationship," was his mother's rejoinder. The next hurdle to overcome was his father.

The Grahams weren't given to histrionics. Matters were handled in a civilized manner. Calm would prevail above the turmoil. Michael later went off to play squash leaving his mother to break the news to his father. When he returned his dad quizzed him on who it was he was seeing and how long this had been going on. Jesse told him, "You are a lot older than she and should have known better. You have endangered both your lives. Surely you realise you can get locked up for this. We talked about you furthering your studies and now you're about to jeopardize everything. You are inexperienced about love, Michael, and naïve to the ways of the world. This is nothing but an infatuation. You have absolutely no future together." Jesse told Michael to break off our relationship immediately and focus on prior plans of doing his Master's degree in England. Michael said he listened to his father in silence as he knew that trying to reason with his father would be a lost cause.

Jesse seldom came into our office. So it took me by surprise when he came to use the Xerox machine that was in the opposite corner to where I sat. I felt the blood whoosh to my face, setting it on fire. I kept my head down, pretending not to notice him. But then curiosity got the better of me. I stole a glance and our eyes momentarily met. Try as I might to get back to my work, it was a losing battle.

That very week, when I was temporarily manning the switchboard for Monica, Michael slipped me an envelope. I was taken aback that it was not his usual note to me but a type-written envelope addressed to him care of Highams. His face looked drawn. He didn't say anything and left immediately. Making sure the coast was clear; I slid the notepaper from the envelope. I had a grave sense of foreboding that this might be the beginning of the end for us.

As I rode home on the bus, I read and re-read the letter. To the best of my recollection it read something like this: *White Boy, we got our eye on you. Kip away frum our kind or els.* It was signed, *from KK (Kensington Killers)* with a sketch of a dagger dripping with blood drawn in red ink. I came to the conclusion that the spelling errors were deliberate, that it was contrived and the sender was someone who obviously wanted to scare Michael off. I'd never heard of any gang by the name Kensington Killers. Gangs invariably had far more fanciful names such as *The Casbahs* and *The Mongrels*. Kensington Killers just didn't ring true. Furthermore, they wouldn't have the smarts to send a type-written note.

I showed the letter to my mother when I got home. She chuckled and said nonchalantly,

"No man, it's only Mr. Graham trying to scare Michael off."

Although Jesse later without a doubt proved himself to be extremely fair and not in the least vindictive, I couldn't help speculating that the letter was written or orchestrated by him as a desperate measure to frighten Michael into ending our relationship.

Chapter 38

Falling Apart

The weeks following the balloon going up at Claverhouse were harrowing. Michael rarely came to the office and with my having no home phone our contact was all but severed. The next thing I heard was that Michael was off to Sibasa, 1300 miles away. I was ill with grief and yearning. I thought that was it and the thought of never seeing him again was too hard to bear. But it wasn't long before a letter from Michael came in the mail:

My dearest Jen,

I know events of the past few weeks have been trying for us both to say least. I have spoken to my parents about us and as I feared they were very upset. My father has suggested that I come up here to Sibasa to help with the stocktaking as well as to think things through more clearly and objectively.

It's all very unfortunate that we happen to live in the only country in the world, which legally prohibits you and I from associating with each other in a manner we would like. The last thing in the world I will ever be is embarrassed or ashamed about our relationship. What we have enjoyed, for all the problems that we've

*encountered, is a decent and precious union. I'm just
sorry it cannot be accepted as such by others.*

*My Sweetheart, perhaps I have not thought through
clearly the logistics of our going to England together. My
mind is in turmoil and perhaps there is merit in my
father's suggestion that I go to England alone, and give
ourselves one year's separation to put our love to the test.
If it has stood the test of time, then it would have a
stronger chance of success. If we're meant to be together,
Jen, our love will prevail.*

Take heart my darling and stay strong.

All my love,

Michael

My worst fears were being realized. This was the final nail
in the coffin.

In the state I was in, how could I possibly think logistically
or logically? I could barely think at all! I saw Michael's
change of plan as desertion and capitulating to his father's
wishes. Was this the way he was going to end our union – at
arm's length, through this letter. A week later, another letter
arrived. He was coming to see me to say goodbye before
leaving for England.

I was a fragile shell when I saw his old Valiant pull up
outside our house. Once inside the lounge, he held out his
arms to embrace me but I rebuffed him as tears coursed down
my cheeks.

"Darling, I hate seeing you so upset."

"Jen, as I said in my letter, I've talked very candidly with
my parents and I think their suggestion about a separation to

put our love to the test would be prudent. Things have been so haywire – and given our strange circumstances - neither of us have had the opportunities to really think things through in the clear light of day. I must agree with my father that it would be wise for us to give ourselves some time."

I swallowed the sob that rose in my throat and uttered, "So what you're saying then is that you're having cold feet?"

"No, my darling, not in the least," he said pleadingly. "Look, I believe that if we're meant to be together, then nothing will stand in our way. It's just…let's not rush into things immediately."

My grief turned to anger.

"Oh, I see now. So Daddy tells you, at age twenty eight, what to do and you do it?"

"Jen, darling, it's not like that at all. It's all equally upsetting for me as well, but please try to understand that we both just need to think things through clearly."

"What's more to think about, Michael? If you're having second thoughts about us, then we may as well end it now. Goodbye, Michael it was very nice knowing you. Have a wonderful life in England," I blurted out, my face contorted with pain as tears spilled over my cheeks.

"Oh my darling, don't get so upset – it pains me to see you this way," he tried to comfort me. "I'm sorry, darling, but I must go now. I have dinner arrangements with my family."

The lump in my throat swelled and my voice choked.

"Just go."

And with that I caught a glimpse of his blurred image disappearing.

I rushed into my bedroom, the walls felt like they were closing in on me. I was overcome with raw sobs. Auntie Una, visiting at the time followed me into the room. "There now, Jenny, don't go upsetting yourself like that," consoled Auntie Una, taking me into her arms. "If it's meant to be, God will surely make a way for you and Michael."

That night I wept till there were not more tears to cry. I went to bed crying and woke up still in morning crying. In the back of my mind I had envisaged things to end this way, but now that it was finally happening, I was apoplectic with the thought of the inevitability of losing Michael and the incredible relationship we had had.

I sobbed the entire weekend and on the Monday morning, I got dressed for work but got only as far as the front door. I desperately needed to get away. If only I could talk to Michael's parents and convince them that I wasn't a horrible person and to plead with them to give us a chance. I made my way to the only neighbours in our area who had a phone. If they noticed my swollen eyes, they didn't say anything. I made my call. Jesse answered. "Can I come see you at your home to talk?" My voice was thin and timid.

"Yes, er…Jenny. I think that would be a good idea. I'd like to talk to you too… Do you know how to get here?"

"Yes," I replied in a low tone, feeling somewhat guilty, like an intruder, about the times I spent in his home in his absence.

I wore my brown tweed skirt and matching top and on my feet I had ungainly looking suede platform shoes, which I hoped Nancy would not find off-putting. I wished I had had more sophisticated looking shoes, but with my budget, it was exactly that – wishful thinking. At *Claverhouse* house, I rang the doorbell and heard the cowbell's hollow jangle. Jesse, clad in his suit and tie, opened the door. His first words to me were "You're not….are you?" He somehow couldn't say the word 'pregnant.' I instinctively understood what he was asking, and wearily answered "no." I was emotionally and physically spent. Nancy, who to me, resembled a 1950s Hollywood film star, hovered in the background as Jesse led the way to the study.

What a contrast to the last time I went into that study. Jesse and Nancy sat in what I assumed to be their familiar armchairs while I took the seat by the door. Gazing at me appraisingly through pale blue eyes under bushy brows, he came straight to the point. "I'm glad that you came to see us," he said, certainly not meaning it in a social context. "It is most unfortunate, Jenny, that we find ourselves in these unpleasant circumstances," he began his soliloquy. "Michael has been extremely irresponsible and should never have pursued this relationship with you. Like it or not, it is a fact that we live in a country with laws such as they are, but besides that, believe me, a relationship such as yours would never work - whether it is here or anywhere else. Mrs. Graham and I have travelled overseas quite extensively, and believe me, there is prejudice all over the world. You are very young still, Jenny, and what you feel for Michael is no doubt infatuation and vice versa." I shook my head from side to side and through sniffles I managed to sputter, "It's not infatuation – we really love each other."

"Be that as it may, sometimes true love requires sacrifice. Sometimes love requires us to relinquish that to which we hold on for the sake of doing what's the right thing to do. If you should go to England, you'll be in a situation where you'll be separated from your family in a strange, cold land. You'll suffer loneliness and homesickness.

Again, as I've said before, there's prejudice all over the world and you may find yourselves isolated and not easily accepted overseas. And when children come into the picture that will compound the problem because they may face rejection. If you truly love each other you'll make this sacrifice for both your sakes. It is best for Michael to be concentrating on his studies at present. You are both very emotionally involved and therefore not thinking clearly and facing the realities of life. We are not in the least prejudiced, but it is a fact of nature that kind marries kind. You have some fine young men among your own people and I'm sure you'll meet someone worthy of you. I've said all that I'm going to say. I wish you luck. I must go now."

Jesse raised his six-foot plus frame from the chair, murmured something to Nancy and disappeared through the study door. I remained static like a lump of lead, numb, with a lap full of damp tissues. Nancy's blue eyes exuded compassion.

"I know what it's like losing someone. We lost a daughter some years ago." Nancy dabbed her eyes with a handkerchief she retrieved from her sleeve. I was touched by her sensitivity and sympathy. I didn't say anything and just let the tears course down my face. Nancy stood up. I followed her cue trailing behind her to the front door. I found no solace in the gentle, winter sunshine as I drove home paralyzed with grief.

The following morning I drove to work still in a state of misery. John Firth who had summoned me to his office, waited for me inside the door. As I entered, I opened my mouth to speak, but nothing came out. Instead, I collapsed into his arms, spilling tears on his gray suit. "Jenny, what happened between you and Michael, shouldn't have. He was irresponsible to have this relationship with you. You're still very young, don't burn your fingers, *loov*," Mr. Firth muttered in his pronounced Lancashire accent. "Take this week off till you feel well enough to come back," he added.

I left his office feeling like I had fallen into a deep, dark pit. Driving home it was all I could do from stemming the dam holding back my sobs. I eased the Valiant into the garage and turned off the ignition. The floodgates opened giving way to hysterical wailing. Ray appeared and yanked the door open.

"Look, enough of this. Pull yourself together. You can never make yourself so sick. No man!" She scolded, her face all piqued. I stumbled into the house and flopped down on my bed like a rag doll.

I woke up the next morning still crying. The glossy, pimply stucco walls of the bedroom felt horribly claustrophobic. I went to my parents' bedroom and bawled, "I want to go away. I just want to go away. Please take me away, I can't stand it here."

"Shame" Ted muttered.

The following day, Ted arranged for me to stay with relatives in the country. My father's cousin, Billy Raatz and his wife, Maude lived in Paarl, the "pearl" of the Berg River Valley, a lush fruit and wine region. As Ted and I drove in silence along the Paarl Road, I stared blankly out of the window, paying scant attention to the attractive gabled farm homesteads nestled amid lush vineyards. The famed oval granite dome of Paarl Rock ahead faintly registered in my mind, but at that moment there was nothing particularly beautiful about this land and its cruel laws.

The sweet country air coupled with Auntie Maude's delicious cooking and warm hospitality was just the remedy I needed to collect my emotions and thoughts. I'm surprised at my maturity at the time. But I came to realize the more I clung to Michael, the worse I was making it for myself.

I had never known a love so unconditional and precious, but perhaps his father was right in saying that sometimes love requires sacrifice - I needed to let him go.

But I needed providential strength. "Dear God, if Michael and I are meant to be together, then please remove the obstacles in our way, and if not, then give me the grace to let him go, and to trust that you have some other plan and purpose for my life." I was also keeping my fingers tightly crossed.

After a week's convalescing under Auntie Maude's care, I returned to Cape Town in a much better frame of mind. I was prepared to give ourselves the one year 'trial' separation that his father had suggested, but prepared myself mentally that time and distance were sure to drive us apart. He would meet an English girl and I would become history - an unfortunate episode in his life.

Having recuperated from the drama of past weeks, I threw myself into my work. Michael was no longer a distraction and things had settled down at the office. Eleanor had left to have her first child and a new girl, fresh out of secretarial school, replaced her. The switchboard kept on buzzing and Mr. Graham still kept to his normal two-mornings per week routine with Monica doing her, "Good Morning, Mr. Graham" part. Word had naturally got out that I had had a dalliance with the boss' son, so whenever I went upstairs through the factory to use the toilet, I would run the gauntlet of fifty pairs of eyes curiously trained on me. I knew there would be whispers and gossip, but I smiled politely and went about my business.

Arriving home one evening, my mother handed me an airmail letter bearing an English postmark. Overjoyed, I ran my hand over the tidy handwriting I'd come to know so well. Michael wrote that he had settled well into university life, that he had bought a red mini station wagon that got stolen and that he missed me desperately. He told me wherever he went, he wished he could share the moment with me. He wrote that while he had talked about a trial separation to put our love to the test, life without me was unbearable. We had the funds for a 'plane fare for me, what with the Jaguar prize money, so there was nothing standing in the way of my joining him, except for his father perhaps. He told me he wrote to his father telling him there'd been a change of plan and he wanted me to come sooner rather than waiting a whole year.

Given latest developments, and his position, Jesse could easily have pulled me aside to put pressure on me to desist, but that's not the kind of man he was. Jesse wanted to talk the matter over with my parents. Whether they felt intimidated by his status, much to my embarrassment, they never responded to his request to meet. I rang Jesse from a phone booth to apologize for their breech of etiquette, coming up with some excuse for them. Sensing irritation in his voice, he reiterated the essence of what he had told me at our meeting at Claverhouse – that there was no future in our relationship. When I responded with "But we truly love each other," he told me, "You're a very persistent young lady!"

A lesser man would probably have pulled rank and had me sacked. Having friends in high places Jesse could have used his clout to prevent my getting a passport. But again he proved himself to be a man of fairness and integrity. He allowed me to remain at Highams and never gave me any indication of displeasure.

Back in Kensington, I kept my eyes peeled on the mailbox for Michael's weekly letters. He instructed me to go to the Thomas Cook travel agent in town. He had arranged the purchase of my ticket through a Thomas Cook branch in England and said the Cape Town branch would help me with my passport application, visa and travel documents. My going to the travel agent was heady stuff. Because of the job reservations law, the ticket agents were white and glamorous.

All dolled up, I felt oh-so-mature and worldly-wise walking into their plush office. I told the pretty blonde agent my name and that my fiancé in England had arranged an airline ticket for me. This was in the era of paper tickets in quadruplicate – resembling a thin booklet the size of a checkbook. She gave me the necessary forms to complete, instructed me to have passport photos taken and bring back the completed documents. I made a mental note to make a trip to Van Kalker Photography in Salt River that just about everyone in Cape Town used. I was to pick up my travel documents ten days or so before my departure on Christmas day.

Over past months I'd been on a rollercoaster ride of emotions and here I was back on top of the world, but far from being out of the proverbial woods. I was still on tenterhooks. This being South Africa, anything could happen. "Please God, don't let the government block my application," I prayed.

Table Mountain. View from
One Sixty Six, Ninth Ave,
Kensington

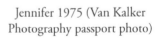

Jennifer 1975 (Van Kalker
Photography passport photo)

Michael 1975 (Van Kalker
Photography passport photo)

Front view of
Claverhouse

Back view of Claverhouse

Claverhouse pool

Table Mountain in classic postcard pose (photo: Basil Dickens)

Graham family on ship to England in 1958

Nancy Graham

Jesse Graham

Jesse Graham WWII soldier
(served in Northern Africa)

Horace and Cecilia
Graham (Michael's
paternal grandparents)

Horace and Cecilia Graham

House in Sibasa

Judith Graham

Christmas Day at D.F. Malan Airport.
(Front L-R) Steven and David (Back
L-R) Sharon, Jennifer and Desmond

Connie, Jennifer and
Sharon (L-R)

Our Wedding Day in
Leeds, England in Mr.
Beal's car.

Jennifer in white velvet gown with
ostrich feather-trimmed hood

Bride and groom with
"surrogate" family

South Parade Baptist
Church, Headingly,
Leeds, England

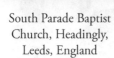

Joyce and David
Green

Michael in the red Mini station wagon

Celebrating our 35th
Wedding Anniversary
at South Parade Baptist
Church 2011 when we
were touring Europe

Ted and Ray
(taken around the
early 90s)

Sharon and Ray (2009)

In loving memory of Cousin Connie who died in
February 2013

Chapter 39

Hope On The Horizon

At the airport, I looked out toward Table Mountain now appearing like a gargantuan granite sculpture on the horizon. In my mind, this would be the last time I'd see this beloved lodestone that had been my daily reference point. I was saying goodbye to stunningly beautiful Cape Town bathed in sunny skies.

In my community, for someone to board a plane was an event. For someone to fly overseas was on another scale entirely. Just going to the airport to watch the planes take off and land, in itself was thrilling. So it was little wonder that close to a hundred relatives and friends came to see me off at D. F. Malan Airport. There I was the centre of attention, dressed to the nines, like a celebrity of sorts.

"Shame, she's brave, hey?" I heard an auntie say.

"Mmm," nodded another one in agreement and wonderment.

"Holly ha, to think she's going all that way by herself to England."

"I know," chimed in yet another. "I'd be so scared."

Fear was the last thing on my mind. I was bursting with excitement and anticipation at the thought of being reunited with Michael in a free land. I had spent the week preceding Christmas packing, unpacking and repacking my brand new suitcase that I purchased with my salary that Ray and Ted, wonder of all wonders, allowed me to keep that month. When Christmas dawned, I had another of those "pinch-me,

so-I- know- I'm- not- dreaming" moments. The day was hot
and I got suitably attired for church, which I would attend
with the family for the last time.

The ladies were resplendent in new clothes topped with
fancy hats and the men all suited and *Brylcreemed*. After
the service, everyone wished me well and the family looked
forward to a hearty feast with Ray's cream-laden trifle for
dessert.

"Are you sure you had enough to eat?" asked Ray, seeing
me picking at my food.

"Shame, are you too excited to eat? I suppose they'll be
serving food on the plane, hey?"

"Yes," I replied, "The ticket says they'll serve dinner and
then breakfast before I get to London."

"Haai, dis wonderlik, ne?" Ray said in wonderment.

I was the first of my family to not only board an airplane,
but to travel overseas, no less. The hours seemed to be
counting down in slow motion. My fashionable corduroy
dress suitable for the English climate, stockings and high-
heeled pumps were in retrospect the most impractical garb
one could ever wear for a long-haul flight. But back then,
everyone dressed up for air travel.

Papa stood behind the wheelchair bearing Mama.
Through misty eyes he told me in a choked voice, "You know,
Jennifer, when you were a little girl, you always said that one
day you were going to England and you were going to marry
an Englishman."

"Your dream came true," Mama said haltingly. "I'll come
visit you." When the boarding announcement came over
the intercom, I bade my goodbyes to weeping faces. At the
gate, I presented my travel documents, turned to wave, then
walked through the door and out across the tarmac toward
the waiting Boeing jet. I never looked back.

I was far too occupied with my novel surroundings to
get sentimental about the small figures that I would possibly

never see again pressed against the airport lounge windows. At Jan Smuts Airport in Johannesburg, I connected to my London flight.

Unlike today where air travel is as commonplace as getting into any vehicle, this new world of flying was beyond excitement for me. I drank in every single detail. A glamorous British Airways hostess flashed me a friendly welcoming smile and ushered me to my seat. Being Christmas Day it was understandable that the plane was virtually empty.

Today, getting a whole row to yourself on a long haul flight would be wishful thinking. There I was with the plane almost to myself, and I was wishing I had people beside me to share my incredible experience. "Wow, fancy providing blankets and pillows," I said inaudibly to myself, and even headphones for audio entertainment. I examined the headphones, wondering if it should be worn like a stethoscope or a headband. I felt woefully self-conscious about fumbling with the gear, even though there was no one around me.

It didn't take long for the crew to shut the door and prepare the cabin for takeoff. As the gigantic silver bird hurtled down the runway, my breathing became shallow as my chest tightened with a sense of awe, wonder and anticipation all rolled into one. "Someone pinch me please, I can't believe this is *finally* happening" I wished I could tell somebody. I marveled at how this impossible hunk of metal the weight of three blue whales, plus thousands of pounds of cargo, thousands of gallons of fuel, thousands of pounds of people plus their luggage, could lift up into the sky. I will forever be in awe at the forces involved in the science of flight.

Once the aircraft had reached its cruising altitude, the attendants trundled down the narrow aisle with turkey dinners, cranberry sauce, vegetables, Christmas pudding and brandy sauce complete with Christmas cracker (a party favour in the English tradition that normally has a charm, a joke and a paper hat.) And those were the days before plastic cutlery and plastic wine glasses – I had the real thing. I deliberated about the paper hat – should I put it on, or shouldn't I? I felt terribly self-conscious and unsure of myself, not knowing the ropes. I had no idea what the protocol was on an airplane. If I needed to use the washroom, could I just get up and go? There I was, a lone figure with a paper hat on my head, tucking quietly into my dinner. It was a strange and marvelous Christmas.

The jet sailed through the dark, velvety stratosphere bound for Nairobi. I felt somewhat alone and apprehensive about this unknown part of Africa. I tensed up about not knowing whether we were to disembark or not. Thankfully the captain announced that we were stopping for a refuel and that we'd shortly be on our way to Frankfurt and then London. Michael had suggested that I fly British Airways because the flight time was shorter than that of South African Airways, which was barred from flying over almost all the African countries, because of its apartheid policies. SAA had to fly around the bulge of Western Africa to get to Europe.

I scrolled through the music channels on the armrest and was thrilled to find my favourite singer. This might sound corny, but it's true. A warm glow engulfed me, and my lips broke into a nostalgic smile as Karen Carpenter's rich, mellow alto piped into my ear, *"Love, look at the two of us, strangers in many ways; We've got a lifetime to say, I knew you well/for only time will tell us so/and love may grow/for all we know."* I hugged the small pillow to my chest and let The Carpenters music usher me into realms of celestial bliss. This, to me, was indeed a good omen that things were meant to be.

During the rest of the flight, I had exhausted all the reading materials to my avail. I managed to fall asleep, albeit restless. At least it brought some respite to my infernal boredom. On Boxing Day morning at around half past six, in a typically grey, wet London, the aircraft finally touched down at Heathrow Airport. After I had cleared customs, I teetered nervously on high heels, feet swollen, wrapped in a Sherlock Holmes style cloak, toward the baggage claim sign. I prayed that Michael would find me in this maze of an airport. My prayer was answered almost immediately. I spotted the unmistakable short, wavy-haired figure of my darling, beside a taller one, heading toward me. At this point, being the hopeless romantic I am, I'd like to report that I kicked off the shackles from my feet, and glided on the air in slow motion toward Michael's open arms. Instead, I wobbled toward him and his companion whom he introduced as Eli. Relief with a capital R was written all over Michael's face. "Oh darling," he said, "I'm so glad you made it safely. I was sick with worry."

Riding in Michael's little red Mini station wagon, the damp, gloomy streets of London were a far cry from the South African sunny skies I had left behind. But that was the least of my worries. For me, snow, rain, hail, whatever didn't matter as long as I was with my beloved. I was wholly fascinated by this new world into which I was being introduced, reveling in the notion that I was so far removed from the horrid bigotry of South Africa and shenanigans of *maison des* Paulses.

My new world now consisted of television, central heating, zebra pedestrian crossings, the London A-Z booklet, underground tubes, ancient brick buildings dating back to Noah, names like Edgeware, and Golders Green and Charing Cross. On New Year's Eve, walking the frigid streets of Hampstead with Michael's university friends, yet again felt like being on a movie set, with the romantic ambience of subdued streetlights reflecting off the wet pavements. Then suddenly disappearing into the bowels of the earth to catch the underground Tube, I turned into Alice in Wonderland.

Michael had reserved a table at a restaurant on a barge docked on a canal somewhere in Camden Town for our group. Lights glistening on this waterway, the restaurant with its crisp linen, the company comprising people from French Canada, Brazil, England and South Africa, were all so magical to me. For the first time in our relationship, Michael and I were able dine out publicly. It felt so strange and what's more, nobody was looking at us suggesting we were doing something wrong. Unless you'd grown up in South Africa during the apartheid years, you'd just not believe how liberating it was to enjoy an occasion like this. I drank in my first taste of freedom like a newborn infant taking its first gulp of air.

When the festive season was over, Michael and I parted company with Eli and his girlfriend, Suzanne. Braving the impossible streets of London, weaving through a labyrinth of ring roads and roundabouts, we finally hit the M1 and set our little red Mini northbound to Leeds. The road ahead for us was long - literally and figuratively – but there was nothing about the future I dreaded. My beloved and I were truly free to love each other without any repercussions.

We stayed at Michael's tiny bed-sit (studio-for-one) with communal bathroom down the hall. The landlord was a no-nonsense Yorkshireman, Mr. Downs, whom I'd not met, but of whom I was nevertheless afraid. Word was that Mr. Downs did not take kindly to live-in guests or any guests for that matter. He might even have been related to Basil Fawlty!

Fortunately, one of Michael's university colleagues and his new bride were vacating their one-bed-roomed flat to move overseas. Number One, Clarendon Road, was where we cozily settled in conveniently located within walking distance of the university. Michael knuckled down to his thesis work while I found a temporary position in a typing pool which I absolutely loathed. But just being together under one roof and not ever having to look over our shoulders was all that mattered to me, although there was something that nagged at me. I was sent off from home with wedding dress in tow with the understanding that there would be no "living in sin."

We both wanted a church wedding. But what church, and where? With Michael's background being Anglican and mine Pentecostal, we decided that a reasonable compromise would be Baptist. Serendipity brought us to South Parade Baptist Church on Kirkstall Lane, Leeds. We were astounded by the reception we received. The congregation was immensely friendly and welcoming, and before long Joyce Green, the pastor's wife invited us to English tea at the manse. This diminutive, white-haired lady was kindness personified and became like a surrogate mother to me. When we expressed our desire to be married, Joyce and her husband, Reverend David Rigden Green arranged the wedding for us.

"Have you thought of what flowers you would like in your bouquet?" Joyce asked.

I'm sure from the blank look I gave her she quickly realized I was as green as a pea about marriage and wedding protocol, because she immediately told me not to worry about a thing and she'd take care of not only my bouquet but also arrange a reception at the manse. When David asked me who would be walking me down the aisle to "give me away," all went quiet. I looked across at Michael for help but all he could manage was a shrug of the shoulders. "I haven't really thought about it," I replied with a nervous giggle.

David then suggested Mr. Beal, one of the deacons, whom we had befriended. "That would be wonderful," I said. Ted and Ray attending the wedding was financially out of the question and I was really quite unsentimental and indifferent about my father not being there to play that role.

And so, on a sunny, but crisp Friday afternoon on March 26, 1976, at South Parade Baptist Church, Mr. Beal, a tall and kindly Yorkshireman, walked me down the aisle. I wore the long-sleeved white velvet, hooded gown with downy ostrich trim, Auntie Freda had made while in my hand I held the pleasingly fragrant bouquet of white roses and yellow freesias, Joyce had put together. I had chosen the fabric and style because I had envisaged England too cold for a traditional bridal gown.

The congregation of about forty friends who became our substitute family for that day, smiled warmly at me as Mr. Booth belted out Wagner's *Here Comes the Bride* on the grand old pipe organ. I was in a daze and found it mindboggling trying to assimilate everything at once. Interestingly, I was quite ambivalent about having no family members present. After the rollercoaster we had ridden, this day was the fulfilment of our dreams.

Michael had written to his parents giving them our wedding date, more by way of a formality than having any expectation of their being there. In his candid response, Jesse wrote that he and Nancy couldn't pretend to be overjoyed and reiterated that we should've given ourselves a year's trial period. However, he did wish us good luck.

Robed in his clerical vestments, David Green, in his clear voice and impeccable diction called us into the holy estate of matrimony. Knowing that our declaration of no "*lawful impediments as to why we should not enter into holy matrimony*" would have an entirely different meaning in South Africa was sobering. Michael and I made our vows to each other: "*I call upon these persons here present to witness that I, Michael Jesse Graham/Jennifer Bridget Paulse, do take thee to be my lawful wedded wife/husband, to have and to hold, from this day forward, for better for worse, for richer, for poorer, in sickness and in health, to love and to cherish, till death us do part, according to God's holy ordinance and thereto I give thee my troth.*"

After the wedding I sent an audiotape of the ceremony back home. Some years later, my sister told me that the whole family had gathered around the kitchen table at my parents' house to listen to it. She said it was quite an occasion. All eyes were focused on the tape recorder as they hung on to every word. There were tears of both joy and sadness. After it was all over, Sharon recalls Papa saying all choked up, "A truer gentleman you've never seen."

"*Haai*, it's like a fairy tale, hey?" was Ray's rejoinder.

Epilogue

October, 1976 was the first time we saw Michael's parents since leaving South Africa the previous year. They invited us to join them for dinner at the Royal York Hotel where they were staying. The last time I had seen them was in their living room under a pall of gloom. The mood in the grand dining room was understandably strained. The "infatuation" they had hoped might blow over was now a union. Conversation revolved around Michael's recently acquired masters' degree, our imminent move to Cambridgeshire where he had secured an engineering job, Graham family members and their mutual friends, none of whom I knew. I barely said a word. Nancy was well aware how awkward things were for me and to her credit she made every effort to put me at ease.

Time is often a great healer and so it was with this relationship. Seeing us happy in our marriage and Michael having a good job was important to them. We were never going to be close and intimate – the way I might have liked it being the touchy-feely sort I am. They were "old school" - colonial in culture and manner, very proper and undemonstrative even when grandchildren arrived in 1977 and 1980. Nevertheless, it was very evident that they thoroughly enjoyed coming to see us on their annual overseas trips.

The riots of 1976 set South Africa on a course of no return. International pressure was brought to bear on the white Nationalist government to dismantle apartheid and offer democracy to all. Domestically they couldn't stem the tsunami of nationwide non-white unrest. Their hand was forced to make some changes. Concessions regarding petty apartheid were the beginning, but in 1986, when I visited South Africa for the first time in ten years, the Immorality Act was still on the statute books. So, I went on my own.

I spent two weeks with Michael's parents and the rest of the month with my family. What a contrast. Jesse and Nancy went out of their way to make me feel part of their family. Nancy took me to meet their friends who were all most welcoming, although I couldn't help feeling their scrutiny of finally meeting the "Coloured" daughter in law.

We went to upscale restaurants by now legally open to all. In reality, few non-whites were able to afford such upper echelon places, so mine was the only brown face among a sea of whites; something that years earlier would have left me feeling uncomfortable, but having lived in a free society for ten years, had little impact on me.

At *maison des* Paulses, what had drastically changed since my leaving were additions to the family. In 1977, I had looked forward to Ray's coming over to England to be with me for the birth of our first child. That was not to be. Her letter had disappointing news; she said she didn't know how it happened, but she was pregnant too! She thought she was going through the "the change of life" and boy, did her life ever change – a double whammy – twin girls.

When friends congratulated me on my baby's birth, "Your mother must be over the moon about her first grandchild," I'd just laugh lamely saying "yes." I know life can be quirky, but how embarrassing is it to tell your friends that your mother is pregnant and that your daughter will be a month older than her aunts! Unfortunately, little else had changed. Ray and Ted's lives muddled along in the same chaotic way as when I left them in 1975 - blaming, sniping and shouting.

July1990 was a time I will always remember. Not solely because it was a Graham family reunion in the United

Kingdom to celebrate Jesse and Nancy's 50th wedding anniversary, but because of what Jesse said at the garden party function held for them at the Highams' home. In his speech, he paid tribute to his daughters in law saying his sons, "married girls of character." That he judged me, to quote Martin Luther King, "by the content of my character and not by the colour of my skin" meant the world to me.

Factory closures and economic down turns precipitated a number of moves in order for Michael to secure worthwhile employment. For the most part I was a stay-at-home mom but did venture into the workforce here and there, doing everything from being an "Avon lady" to food caterer to teacher's aide in a school library. I also took full advantage of continuing education opportunities. My studies at McGill University, Montreal, were interrupted after three semesters when Michael's job transferred us from Cornwall, Canada to Mobile, Alabama.

What a culture shock! But fortunately all was not lost. My McGill credits enabled me to enrol at Mobile University as a full time student. Graduation day was doubly memorable. Not only was I thrilled to be getting my Bachelor's degree in Communication/Journalism, but having my name announced as the recipient of a scholastic award for the female student who had made the most progress during her course of study was one of my proudest moments.

On our return to Canada in 2011 after nine wonderful years in New Zealand (but that's another story), we made a detour via Leeds, England to be there for March 26, our 35th wedding anniversary. Having our picture taken in front of the altar where we had made our vows decades ago, seemed so far removed - like another lifetime.' In three decades our world has changed radically in terms of technology, communications and social attitudes. Thankfully, apartheid is dead. Our love prevailed and our story continues.

Glossary

agh	oh (agh pronounced with a guttural g sound)
baas	boss/master (term usually used by non-whites toward whites)
blerrie	corruption of bloody
bobotie	Malay influenced sweet, sour and spicy meat dish
boekies	picture books
bokkie	darling
boytjie	small boy
bredie	stew
bubbie	male Indian shopkeeper
dagga	marijuana
deurmekaar	harum-scarum
dikbek	pout
donner	a beating
dorp	village
dronkies	drunks
frikadel	fish or meat patty
haai	expression of surprise
hartjie	little heart
holly-ha	Expression of surprise
ja	yes
joll	to hang out with; and/ or have an extra-marital affair
juffrou	miss
kaffir	derogatory term for black

kakbalie	shit barrel
kind	child
klap	smack
klein	small
klopse	street performing minstrels
kool	cabbage
koppies	cups
kroeskop	Afro-textured hair
kwaai	fierce
lang tafel	long table (extra tables added for a large gathering)
lat	switch
lekker	delicious
mal	crazy
meneer	mister
mevrou	missus
mielie pap	maize porridge
Monkey nuts	peanuts
motjie	female Indian shopkeeper
nee	no
Oe Here	Oh Lord
padkos	food for the road
pens en pootjies	tripe and pigs trotters
pesella (bonsela)	a small gift (
plaas	farm
pondokkie	shack
sinkdak	corrugated iron roof
skel	scold
skelm	dishonest
skinner	gossip
skollie	hoodlum
stukkie	small piece
verdomde	damned
verjooltjie	small violin
vetkoek	deep-fried dough rounds

vlei	wetlands
voorkamer	front room (living room)
vrou	woman

Appendix

Some of the notes Michael wrote me:

1974

Love, Missed you very much this weekend Could you possibly come home with me after work to our new cottage & have a bite of supper — please love as I've missed you so. If it's okay let me know before lunch as I'll be taking most of the afternoon off to buy provisions etc. & will be back probably shortly before five

1974 —

± 11.30pm

Dearest Jen

note which will   short
a first the bad   read like
the good news   then

      Not bad news really —
Just a mild lecture from
your very own Uncle Michael!
Seriously love, I hope your
stomach improves — are you
eating any lunch these days
I know you didn't the other
day — well that's not being
sensible at all my girl.
Please love, it's important that
you eat properly, even if
you only have something very
light at lunch it is essential
to eat at least something So
if you want to upset me
then don't listen to what I
say That way I'll know how
much you care about my
concern over you

I was going to tell you
a joke but when written
on paper it
at all amusing
have to tell you
sometime
    I've just been listening
to a record which had
a line saying " I've
got lots of empty time
to spend and wish
you could be here" Well
I'm not so sure about having
all that amount of empty
time at my disposal but I'm
pretty certain about the last
part of the verse, which is
my way of saying that I could
think of nothing nicer than
having you here with me to
keep me warm while we drift
off into dreamland I'm just going
to read a short scientific article
in Time Magazine which looks to
be rather interesting — then it's off
to sleep and dreams about a certain
young lady

1974

Hi love,

Having searched
in vain for my clip-board
on which I intended
writing this short work of
art I have had to resort
to adopting a more accustomed
pose — namely sitting at
a desk!

I happened to overhear
snatches of your tea time
conversation (I know, don't
say it, it's rude to eavesdrop)
concerning the pros and cons
of moving out of home.
Eleanor offers some very
matronly but probably very
sound advise in saying that
it's as well not to be too
hasty in one's decision

My mind somewhat
restless right now and full
of wild dreams and ideas.
I'd like to, as you
would say, fly away with

you to a Swiss chalet
high in the Alps with
the snow lying deep all
around outside and the
two of us all cosy
round a beautiful log
fire. And slowly we'd
learn more about eachother
and I'm sure grow even
more fond of one another.
     But unfortunately we
live in a real and not
a dream world.
     I'm rather apprehensive
and nervous about seeing
your Mum tomorrow —
however I'll have to cross
that bridge when I come to
it. I hope she doesn't ask me
how our whole affair started
cause then I'll be at a bit
of a loss for something to say.
     The worst thing of all
is going to be to have to say
that I won't see you
again (other than in working

(3)

hours of course), for I'm
sure she's bound to ask
me to do this.

And my reason for
this note? None at all
other than enjoying any
form of concact I can
make with you —
i.e. it's just an excuse
to perhaps get some
sort of a reply from
you (if I'm lucky) to
do my heart and ego
good!

Nº 164

My love,

    I'm terribly sorry, it does seem as though things have become very involved. It's always easy to look back and say, or rather realise where one went wrong. I guess that point was on our first meeting at which time I should have said — "Jenny there's no future in it, let's leave it before things go too far." Easy to say now — not so easy to do them. Anyhow, we can't dwell on what should have happened, we must face the situation as it actually is.

    The thought of, well not quite

'losing' you, but rather bringing
an end to our relationship
gives me nothing to feel very
happy about.

I very much wanted to
see you tonight My people
are out of town till tomorrow
& I was going to suggest you
come home for a meal. However
things have now occurred which
look to make this impossible.

Your mother is quite right, were
I in her shoes I would also
like to see who was taking my
daughter out — especially under the
circumstances where it is quite unthinkable
for her to imagine I am taking advantage
of you — the law being that it is and
my having the supposed right colour then
Please love, don't look so sad, it
upsets me; we will have to discuss it
all and come to some decisions Write me ...

Jennifer,

Being in the frame of mind I am right now I don't think it's worth my while talking to your Mom — at least not at the present time as I don't think I'll be very clear in my arguments just at the moment.

I'm sorry I've upset your parents so much — I'm very disturbed by your Dad's reaction although, I can well understand his feelings. I'm certain he feels that you and I were far more involved physically than what actually transpired. For as far as I'm concerned and I always will be of this opinion, there was nothing at all in our relationships of which one could be ashamed. Furthermore, what we enjoyed together I think only you & I will ever understand — and I'm afraid that 99% of the people would probably agree with your father in thinking that our association can only throw a bad light on his name.

I only hope that you can slowly patch up what is obviously a very great rift between you & your parents And I can't agree with you when you apologise to me for getting me into this whole mess — remember you can't do things on your own — as the saying goes 'it takes two to tango — and I was just as much to blame as you were — in fact far more so.

I would have told you the essence of what I've said above had I gone to the bank with you. However it appears you preferred not to go with me — well I guess that's some

(The last sentence omitted reads "I guess that's something I'll have to accept)

Correspondence from Michael to his mother:

Sibaga
18/8/75

Dear Mom,

Thanks for the letter & your advice. I do concede I have been living a life of deception this last year. This you no doubt realise was to spare you & Dad worrying about it. But probably more than anything it was a case of knowing how Dad would react coupled with the fact that I would like to make a few decisions of my own. You must surely realise how undermining it is to tell people or intimate to them that the real reason you don't want to do this or that is because your father wouldn't like it, especially when you're close to 29. Sure I'm naive & inexperienced in many things but what you probably don't appreciate is how strongly I've wanted to do a few things on my own without having them suggested to me all the time. I'll go overseas and try to lead as full a life as possible and ask God as to what course in life is best for me to pursue.

As regards Jenny — well, I certainly can't change my feelings towards her just like that & have no cause to. She's a wonderful girl and I think that after her initial breakdown — which was very natural under the circumstances — I think she has shown a maturity beyond her years. We both appreciate the situation as it is and accept that if God wishes us to part and go our own separate ways then that's the best for both of us, however upsetting it might be at the time. Whatever might become of our relationship, whether we write or not I'm certain that God brought us together for some reason and I can assure you we're both far better people for the experiences we've enjoyed thus far. I look at that threatening letter as a sign to tell me to move on and start building for the future, not to hang around and procrastinate. I intend to go and say goodbye to Jen & her folks before I leave. I think we'd both like to part under better circumstances and if we both have enough faith in God then we'll be quite happy to part and allow God to point out what courses are best for us to follow. For as she said — so often God's appointments are man's disappointments.

See you next week Mom. Pleased to hear the word from Leeds and am really looking forward to a years study plus seeing Ian again.

Love Richard P.T.O.

This is verbatim correspondence from Jesse to Michael in October 1975.

25/10/75

Dear Michael,

We all agreed that a separation at this stage would be a good thing in that if it stood the test the probability of a successful union would be so much more certain. You yourself said it would be at least twelve months. We understood that you explained this to Jenny. In arriving at your decision have you given yourself sufficient time? Could your change of mind –understandably so- not be rash and impulsive due to initial loneliness and adapting to a new environment? In a few months when you are more settled you might view it in a different light and realize that your first decision was the right one.

We don't know what Jenny's feelings are about going over immediately are but her decision in the matter is more important than yours as she certainly has more to lose than you if it does not work out. I feel as Mom does – that she should at least spend the festive season at home. You are 29 and on your own – the decisions are yours but we are both always more than happy to discuss any points or problems you might have and offer advice for what it is worth.

The question of a mixed marriage is a very complex and involved subject particularly when you are both South African subjects, due to our unique legislation, so I thought it my last duty to give you a complete picture of the legal aspects for your future guidance in the event of actual marriage. I will be posting you this information in a few days' time.

What has been pointed out very strongly is that in a case such as yours the trial period should be much longer than norm in order to be very sure should there be a marriage. In your case divorce without children is very difficult and always a long drawn out procedure in English law – can take years. Divorce with children would be a tragedy for her. S.A. might not allow the child into the country. However, I am sure you know and are conscious of all these things, but nevertheless I feel better about pointing out whatever I can in case you have not given certain things the thought they require. Should any points arise out of this letter write and let me know. Communication, especially in times such as these, is so important and I hope you will air your feelings and problems quite openly so we can give you our honest thoughts and advice for what they are worth.

All well here. It's Mom's birthday today and we are having a bridge party tonight.

Love,

Dad

Michael replied:

30/10/75

Dear Dad

Thank you for your last letter. I was aware of the fact that you would probably feel my decision to ask Jennifer over rather premature. I concede that loneliness and yearning probably come into the reckoning to some degree but are by no means predominant. I did say that we would perhaps give ourselves a 12-month break but in making that statement I was probably not being entirely honest with you or myself. I'm afraid that it was said more in fear than truth.

However your reaction to my plans does fill me with great joy. I have wrongly and through lack of faith I know, been very worried that you might try to stand in our path and use all sorts of means to prevent our coming together. I hope you will forgive me for thinking this way. You have taken a great pressure off me and for the first time in my life I can now feel at ease to discuss difficulties and problems with you; and even if you don't agree with my ideas, will not be scared to voice them for fear of your blocking them but rather to know that you will try and guide and let me make the final choice. I did want Jen to come over early December but she said in all fairness and in light of the help Mr. Firth has given her it would be better that she stayed till the end of the year. I think she's right and her sentiments commendable. We have great trials and tribulations ahead of us I'm sure — you pointed out some of these to me,

*but we happen to be very compatible and determined to
make things work out for us.*

Love,

Michael

Michael's father still understandably had grave reservations about our plans and made one last-ditch effort to dissuade him from marrying me:

12 December 1975

Dear Michael,

Thank you for your letter. Re you and your future, you know my feelings in the matter. I believe that in this life one could choose a wife from more than one person and be absolutely happy. I am sure that had I not met Nan I could have found someone else who would have been a fine wife and made a 100% marriage.

In your case, I think if your trial leads to permanency it can never be 100% for either of you as there will always be a vital side of life missing. Unfortunately I think you will find that you will drift away from both families due to circumstances that happen to exist at present and even if things change here during the coming years it will still take a considerable time for colour adjustments to settle down.

When people have been conditioned for as long as we have these things do not change overnight. You are both isolating yourselves from the country of your birth and possibly from certain friends both here and in other countries. I realize that you have thought of all these things but I am mentioning a few of them for the last time. I have no intention of raising any of these matters again as I don't think anything is achieved by doing so.

Naturally Mom and I are very sad about it all. We had looked forward to your later years especially after the past ten years or so. As a small or younger boy you always said you would marry an English girl. How overjoyed we would have been had you come back with someone we could all enjoy with the added joy of grandchildren. I cannot deceive you by not saying that I pray each and every day that this will still happen. If it doesn't then our respective paths will unquestionably grow further apart and many links will fade. Here's hoping this will not be.

Remember Michael that should the trial indicate that it is not to be, your Mom and I will always be waiting for your return with warmth and much love. I hope you enjoy your Xmas and that the New Year brings responsible and wise decisions to you both. Remember you are so much older and have so much less to lose when compared with her. Mom and I will spend Xmas with Roger quietly at home. We will be thinking of you. I understand that she flies over on the 25th and meets you in London.

Love

Dad

Michael sent his parents a telegram on our wedding day.

POST OFFICE TELEGRAPHS — POSKANTOORTELEGRAAFDIENS T 27

This form and envelope should accompany any enquiry.
Hierdie vorm en koevert moet alle navrae vergesel

RECEIVED
ONTVANG

No.

LEEDS 9 26 1150

CTF161 JCY610 GJB527 BDF839 TT965 SACN CO GBBD 009

GRAYHAM CLAVER HOUSE GLOUCESTERAVENUE

BISHOPSCOURT CAPETOWN

WEDDING TODAY MICHAEL

CTF161 *557-8616 CLT BBB

This is the only correspondence my father ever had with me. After I had written him numerous letters and receiving no reply, I became quite upset and told him in my last letter if I didn't hear from him, I'd take it that he simply doesn't care. This was his response:

DEAREST JENNIFER (1) 1- 6 94

I~am~writing~this I IS WITH DEEP LOVE AND CONCERN THAT I AM WRITING THIS LETTER, FORGIVE ME FOR NOT RESPONDING SOONER. PLEASE DO NOT JUDGE ME TOO HARSHLY IN ASSUMING THAT I DONT SEEM TO CARE ABOUT YOU PERHAPS IF I AM MORE OPEN AND FRANK' YOU MIGHT LEARN AND UNDERSTAND ME WITH DIFFERENT PERSPECT HAVING been A SON OF A LABOURER AND OF COULOR IN THIS COUNTRY HAS NEVER been A bed OF ROSES HOWEVER MY PARENTS REARED ME IN HARD TIMES TO THE best OF THEIR ABILITY

I ALWAYS AS A CHILD HAD AMBITION AND DREAMS FOR THE FUTURE IN SPITE OF OUR PLIGHT AND SITUATION I WANTED TO be A SCHOOL TEACHER but WAS ROBBED OF THE OPPERTUNITY I WAS ONLY ALLOWED TO HAVE PASSED STD 6 because OF FINANCIAL NEED IN THE FAMILY I had TO GO AND WORK THAT HAS been A GREAT DESSAPOINT To me NEVERTHELESS I HAD TO LIVE WITH THAT I had NO CHOICE. I WAS ONLY SIXTEEN THEN I NEVER REALY MADE A SUCCESS OF WHAT EVER EMPLOYMENT THAT FOLLOWED FRUSTRATION CONFUSION SETTLED IN FOUR TIME I CONSIDERED SUICIDE. I DID NOT KNOW THE LORD AT 21 YRS I HAD TO GET MARRIED SOMETHING I WAS NOT PREPARED FOR I LOVED YOUR MOTHER AND WAS COMMITED MY VOWS I HONOURED beFORE THE LORD I UNDERSTOOD SWEET LITTLE About LIFE, AND ITS PITFALLS I LEARNED THE 'HARD WAY SIX CHILDREN WERE bORN AT SHORT INTERVALS

2

MY TASK NOW WAS EVEN GREATER TRYING TO MAKE
ENDS MEET HOW I WISH THINGS COULD HAVE BEEN
DIFFERENT AT 24 YRS THE LORD JESUS SAVED ME
THAT I BELIEVE WAS THE TURNING POINT IN MY LIFE,
FOR WE KNOW THAT ALL THINGS WORKS TOGETHER FOR
GOOD TO THEM THAT LOVE THE LORD TO THOSE THAT ARE
CALLED TO HIS PURPOSE ROM 8-28   PERHAPS
TO MY CHILDREN I MIGHT NOT HAVE BEEN AN AFFECTIONATE
AND IDEAL FATHER BUT I REARED YOU IN FEAR AND THE
NURTURE OF THE LORD AND LOVED YOU ALL VERY DEARLY
ONLY GOD KNOW THAT IS THE TRUTH. I DID THE
BEST FOR YOU UNDER CIRCUMSTANCES AND NEVER
DESERTED YOU

NOW THAT I HAVE LEVELED WITH YOU AND FILLED YOU
IN ON THINGS YOU WERE IMGNORANT TO YOU MIGHT UNDERSTAND
I HAD MY FAIR SHARE OF THE TRIALS OF LIFE IS
DRUDGERY AND SHAM.

I WILL ALWAYS BE ETERNALY INDEBTED TO THE LORD
FOR HIS FAITHFULNESS AND SAVING GRACE FOR
GIVING MEANING TO LIFE AND DETERMINED OUR
DESTINY

         GOD BLESS
           DAD

PS
THIS LETTER I WROTE AT 2. AM

DISCUSSION QUESTIONS
FOR BOOK CLUBS

1. Did the book cover make an impression on you? If yes, what impression? If no, why not?

2. How does the author's description of Cape Town and/ or South Africa affect you? Is it a place you would wish to visit?

3. What characters in the book are you drawn to and why?

4. What themes or motifs are threaded throughout the book?

5. What struck you about the author's psychological state during childhood in creating her imaginary family?

6. Discuss the author's naiveté about sex during that era.

7. What did you find disturbing about the memoir?

8. What made it difficult for people of colour as a whole to embrace education as their means of salvation from their tyranny?

9. How were people of colour in South Africa politically more disadvantaged than those in America before the Civil Rights Movement?

10. Does the book arouse curiosity about South Africa's history, Nelson Mandela, the apartheid ideology or stories about other people's experiences about apartheid and societal racist attitudes in general?

SUGGESTED READING

Long Walk To Freedom, Nelson Mandela

Tomorrow Is Another Country, Allister Sparks

Cry, The Beloved Country, Alan Paton

Kaffir Boy, Mark Mathabane

African Women, Mark Mathabane

July's People, Nadine Gordimer

The Lying Days, Nadine Gordimer

My Traitor's Heart, Rian Malan

The Anglo-Boer War, Fransjohan Pretorius

Disgrace, J M Coetzee

The Heart of Redness, Zakes Mda

Fools and Other Stories, Njabulo Ndebele

A Dry White Season, Andre Brink

CPSIA information can be obtained at www.ICGtesting.com
Printed in the USA
LVOW01s2101060114

368314LV00025B/1185/P